The Lina Fat Cookbook

Recipes from the
Fat family Restaurants
by Lina Fat

with Elaine Corn & Jan Nix

The Crossing Press, Freedom, CA 95019

Cover design by AnneMarie Arnold
Cover photograph by Brooks Photo
Makeup by Jeanne Marie
Back cover photograph by Cathy Kelly

Book design by Amy Sibiga
Interior illustrations ©1992 by Amy Sibiga
Interior photographs: Cathy Kelly—California Fats Restaurant
(pp. 21-22), D. Salladay—Fat City (pg. 21)
Printed in the U.S.A.

Every effort has been made to locate copyright owners and to secure permissions for material used in this book.

Library of Congress Cataloging-In-Publication Data
Fat, Lina, 1938—
    The Lina Fat cookbook : recipes from the Fat family restaurants /
    by Lina Fat with Elaine Corn and Jan Nix.
    p.   cm.
    Includes index.
    ISBN 0-89594-562-2 (cloth) — 0-89594-563-0 (paper)
    1. Cookery, Chinese. 2. Fat, Lina 3. Fat family.
    I. Corn, Elaine. II. Nix. Janeth Johnson. III. Title.
    TX724.5.C5F38 1992
    641.5'09794'54—dc20   92-16742
                                                 CIP

This book is dedicated to my family: my husband Ken, and my children, J.C., Kevin, and Diana. Thank you for being patient.

My deepest gratitude to the Fat family for providing me the opportunity to grow and excel in the culinary profession. A special thank you to my father-in-law, Frank Fat, for his vision, his inspiration, and his trust in me to do a good job; my brother-in-law, Tom Fat, who came back to join the restaurant business, believed in the China Camp project, and ultimately changed my destiny; my sister-in-law, Chee Fat, who supported my original ideas for China Camp and expanded on them by creating names for our dishes; and my niece, Corinne Fat, for being truthful about my flourless cake failure which became the catalyst for my second career.

To my chef, Eric Beamesderfer, I owe a special thanks for his cooperation and creative contributions, and to the management staff, kitchen crew, and service staff in Fat City and California Fats Restaurant for their dedication in maintaining our standards of high quality.

For opening doors to the world of cooking—from West to East—thanks to my roommate, Faye Eubank, and friends, Janie and Sharon, at David Lipscomb College for teaching me to cook my first American dish, the Sloppy Joe; to my childhood friend, Philo, for introducing me to my first peanut butter sandwich; to Doris for helping me cook my first Chinese dish; to my American mother, Carlotta, for introducing me to grilled cheese sandwiches and baked chicken; to my friend Toom, who first taught me about Thai cooking; and to the late Mrs. Chan, founder of Yank Sink Restaurant in San Francisco, who gave me my first lesson in Chinese cooking.

To my friends and family who served as sounding board and tasters when I tested recipes, I am indebted for your honest evaluations.

Most of all, I want to thank my friends who encouraged and supported me through good and bad times. You are my extended family!

Foreword

The first time I interviewed Lina Fat, I called her about the subject of chop suey. With historical and cultural meaning behind my questions—where did it come from, and why—I picked up the phone. From Lina, I got a recipe for chop suey the Fat family eats for Chinese New Year. She gave me its translation—miscellaneous scraps—and discovered that it truly is eaten in Canton to avoid wasting food, and that it's always a little bit different depending on what's on hand and who's behind the wok.

Lina further suggested that I call an American-born Chinese chef with a master's degree in psychology. His name was David SooHoo. She said he might be able to help me with chop suey's newest heights, perhaps give me a history lesson about chop suey's popularity in America at the little Chinese diners opened by Cantonese immigrants.

There was no way we could have known, but Lina had just sent me to meet my future husband. David's relationship with Lina's family went back fifteen years. He had been the martial arts teacher of Lina's sons. When our wedding approached and my own mother, who lives in Texas, was too far away to help with details, it was Lina who went with me to select my wedding dress. With a wedding in Sacramento and a honeymoon departure from San Francisco the next day, a limousine rolled up to the reception and whisked us to the Bay Area, courtesy of Lina and Ken Fat.

It's often difficult to sustain continuity with friendships with people in the restaurant business. They work when most people don't. Lunch. Dinner. Weekends. The hours are long. They stay in one place—the restaurant—all day and night. They have to trust their friends that they understand the friendships are alive, despite little time for nurturing them. When an opportunity to show fondness arises, it comes on strong to balance out the missed opportunities.

It's the balance that makes sense of Lina Fat. Spontaneous menu creations come from quick thought, but after careful analysis. Busy schedules are offset by a few days relaxing in the mountains. Sweet balances sour. Salt balances spice. The bounce of Fat City balances the beauty of California Fats.

As you flip from appetizer to entree, dessert to dim sum, you'll taste your way through the culinary background of Lina's global experiences. The food is as eclectic as she is, yet sensible and delicious. You may not use these recipes every day. To me, the collection is like the good friend you don't see often, but who bridges time the minute you do—like Lina herself, a keeper.

—Elaine Corn

Contents

Introduction by Elaine Corn

A Flourless Chocolate Cake

The whole Fat family was there. With Frank Fat, the founder of Frank Fat's restaurant in the heart of downtown Sacramento, was his wife, Mary. Both came from China, theirs being the long-lasting union of an arranged marriage. Around the table were their first son, Wing, his wife, Chee, and their three children. There were the Fats' two daughters, and their third and fourth sons.

The second-oldest son, Ken, was driving in from San Francisco. He was bringing his new wife, an immigrant from Hong Kong named Lina. Twenty-two years old, she was a few courses shy of a doctorate in pharmacy. He was almost out of dental school.

Because family affairs at Frank Fat's house were always big everyone helped by bringing a dish. Lina's assignment was dessert. Lina was intimidated, considering the size of the group and the superb Chinese and American dishes that usually covered the table. "I wanted to make a cake," she remembers. But she was a terrible cook. During the five years she had lived in America, she had experimented with such native cuisine as Sloppy Joes, hamburgers, spaghetti, and chicken rolled in Rice Krispies, but never a cake.

Lina believed she could do it, though. "After all, I was a pharmacy student. I thought, no problem. I would just buy a cookbook. I bought the *New York Times Cookbook* and found a recipe for a flourless cake with fudge frosting. I knew I could follow a recipe. It is very much like a pharmaceutical formula."

She thought she followed the directions exactly, "but I didn't know that I shouldn't peek in the oven, or that I should use a clean beater for the eggs. I didn't know how stiff stiffly beaten egg whites are. I didn't do anything right, except the frosting. Ken was hurrying me, so I took the cake out of the oven before it was done. On the way to Sacramento, the cake fell. I didn't know what to do. I really wanted to impress the family."

With no time to stop for a bakery substitute, Lina served her cake as it was. No one spoke. Lina understood all too well what silence meant at a Chinese family table where everyone had chattered about food the whole meal long. Finally, her five-year-old niece, Corinne, blurted out, "Auntie Lina, your cake is really good, but it is sure hard."

Lina took a long breath of resolve. "I swore to myself I would learn how to cook until I became the best cook in the family."

That was thirty years ago. Today everyone agrees that Lina Fat is the best cook in the family. Not bad for someone whose culinary repertoire included nothing more than America's more embarrassing classics until she was almost thirty years old.

Before that, Lina hadn't needed to cook. But she knew good food when she tasted it. "In Hong Kong, they teach you how to eat," says Lina.

It Was Supposed to Be Linda

Lina Fat was born Po Ying Yue, "little butterfly," in Hong Kong in 1938. She also had an English name, Linda. But when she started school she couldn't pronounce it. She tried to spell it, but couldn't remember what came between the n and the a. She wrote her name as Lina, and Lina it remained.

Like most of the Chinese in Hong Kong, Lina's parents were of pure Cantonese descent. The people of Canton, China's southernmost province, are said to be dogged, business-minded, and risk-taking. They also claim culinary superiority—based on their fresh ingredients, delicate sauces, and subtle flavors—over all the other regional cuisines of China.

Lina's upbringing was middle-class. Although her father had gone to school in England and worked for the British Motor Company most of his life, the family never ate Western food at home, only Chinese food.

At the time of Lina's birth, Hong Kong had been overrun by the Japanese. When she was still a baby the family fled north to Guilin. There her father bought a share in a restaurant where the famous dish of the area, Yeung Shu Fried Rice, came speedily from the kitchen's woks. But with planes flying menacingly low overhead, business was slow.

A year went by, and the family needed money. Lina's mother, Wong Yuk Ping, was brave and creative in the face of adversity. As Lina remembers, "she bought cigarettes in Guilin. Her plan was to return with them to Canton and sell them for a profit. Had she been caught, she'd have been killed." Yuk Ping managed to avoid detection a couple of times. But then the Japanese came to Guilin, and Lina's parents took her to the family's tiny ancestral village in the Sunwui district of Canton. Lina later found out that the street where her father's restaurant had stood had been bombed. They never went back to Guilin.

Soon the Japanese came to the village and raided it for rice and chickens. The family fled to the mountains. To survive, they boiled sweet potato leaves with tree bark for soup and ate it with rice or whatever grain they could find.

After the war, the family returned to Hong Kong, and Lina's father resumed his job with the British Motor Company. Lina's life came under the strict control of her strong-minded mother. There was no play time, no visits with friends—only studying. Lina's mother hired two tutors for her, one for math and one for English, the most important subject, to her mother's mind. Yuk Ping even bribed her daughter to study hard, promising Lina a watch if she made first in her class. Lina earned the watch—and got her first birthday party and a new dress with it.

When Lina was twelve, her mother died of cancer. With no brother or sister and with a father who ate business dinners in restaurants several times a week, Lina found herself alone with the cook much of the time. But her mother's passing gave her the freedom she desperately needed. Soon she was spending her afternoons with friends, visiting teahouses and having dim sum and Western desserts at Hong Kong's ritziest hotels.

Every day after her mother died, Lina walked home with her girlfriends from St. Paul's Convent, where she attended Catholic high school. They would stop for four o'clock tea, ordering the best shrimp toast Lina can remember. Sometimes she would have a red-bean crush, a popular Hong Kong beverage made from cooked red beans blended with sugar. They also ate finger sandwiches or noodles.

At home, meals were still thoroughly Chinese. Breakfast consisted of congee, a gruel of rice cooked in water for hours and flavored with preserved turnip and dried shrimp. Lunch was two or three dishes—vegetables, fish or meat with rice, and soup. If she didn't go home for lunch, the cook brought food to her at school. Dinner preparations were more elaborate, and included fish, vegetables, meat, rice, and always soup.

Looking back on those days, Lina can't remember ever passing many hours without food. She recollects that she ate all day, although she weighed less than eighty pounds.

During the same period, Lina was learning about the West. By the time she was fifteen she had danced the jitterbug, ridden a Harley-Davidson, joined a bicycle club, gone boating, and developed an addiction to Western movies. To satisfy a longing for Western fashions, she subscribed to *Seventeen*. She had already devised ways to dress up her Catholic school uniform—by adding extra pleats in the skirt, or tying colorful ribbons onto the uniform's regulation bodice. She loved clothes, and still does.

The new distractions in Lina's life didn't keep her from studying—studying hard, just as her mother had directed. But now Lina wondered what she was studying for. "My mother wanted me to excel, but for what? She expected me to get married and stay home."

Not only would Lina not stay at home, she would leave Hong Kong for good. The fashion magazines and Marlon Brando movies had worked their magic. She wanted to come to America. But her mother's influence ensured that her ambitions were practical: she would study to become a pharmacist.

A boyfriend had already left for David Lipscomb College in Nashville, Tennessee. Lina asked her father if she could go to college in America too, but he said it was too expensive. Her grades were excellent, so Lina applied for a scholarship and for work.

She qualified scholastically, but there were other requirements. Her father had to come up with four years' tuition in advance, plus enough money for Lina's return trip, and deposit the entire amount in an account that bore no interest. He obliged.

Lina's job? She was to be a typist in the David Lipscomb College admissions office. There was only one problem: she didn't know how to type. So her father gave her a typewriter, and she practiced on the boat sailing to America.

Lina came to America as part of a modern wave of Chinese immigrants seeking degrees, not gold. But she later came to see herself as one more Chinese newcomer in a long stream of millions, all of whom had crossed the Pacific Ocean on their dreams.

The Gold Mountain

More than 110 years before Lina Fat would become a naturalized citizen of the United States, Chinese laborers, almost all of them Cantonese, flocked to the American West to labor in the mines and on the railroad tracks.

The culture of the Celestial Empire wasn't one of conquest. Most Chinese peasants, in fact, had spent their entire lives in the villages where they were born. But in the 1840s disastrous events in China coincided with new attractions in America. Poverty, drought, and famine caused homelessness and starvation. Two opium wars and the Tai Ping Rebellion, an uprising against marauding Manchu soldiers, brought chaos and terror to southern China. Then came a ruinous flood in 1849. Many Cantonese were ready to seek a better life elsewhere.

When gold was discovered in 1848 at Sutter's Mill, not far from Sacramento, Americans went crazy with gold fever. When the news traveled to Hong Kong and into Canton Province, the glee was not containable. The Chinese believed literally that gold was spilling down the mountains and into the streets, just waiting to be pocketed.

Suddenly, people who had never traveled beyond their villages began to contemplate crossing the vast Pacific Ocean, almost as if such a journey were as inconsequential as a trip to the market. First in line were the men of Canton—from Toisan district, Frank Fat's ancestral district of Hoi Ping, and Lina's parents' district of Sunwui. They left a land of rocky, barren soil, and a life of meager agriculture and fishing, in the hopes of reaching the *gim san*—the Gold Mountain.

In one of the best get-rich-quick schemes ever, shipping companies offered the Cantonese their passage on credit. Buy now, strike gold, pay later.

To the gold seekers, it didn't matter that they would be working for people who wore short hair and beards, spoke an odd language, and drank and fought. Mine owners promised American hospitality and big houses, as well as big pay. Even if life in California turned out less pleasant than imagined, a Chinese man could make his fortune on the Gold Mountain, go home rich, and retire.

After a three-month voyage in the suffocating stench of a ship's hold, sleeping on shelves instead of beds, the Chinese men were deposited at the port of San Francisco, from where they traveled to Sacramento, the gateway to the Gold Country. From Sacramento's tiny waterfront, they fanned out over America's most rugged mountain range—the 400-mile-long, 80-mile-wide chain of granite block known as the Sierra Nevada.

The Chinese were good at ferreting out gold. The secret was to find ore near a stream or river. Water easily washed away the earth in the mining pans, leaving only the precious nuggets. If a miner was lucky, he found a vein, a thick golden streak that looked like a sandwich of gold meat neatly laid between two pieces of hard white granite.

Even in the raw, gold sparkled through the dirt. Experienced and novice miners alike went a little crazy at this sight, as they stood there dirty and tired, imagining a life of riches.

As relatives back in the villages began receiving packages of gold nuggets and dust from the mines, more and more exaggerated stories about the Gold Mountain spread. More Chinese decided to go to America. Peasants and scholars boarded boats together, the Gold Mountain their destiny, gold their great equalizer.

The Chinese Must Go

The Chinese population in California swelled quickly. By mid-1852, Chinese in the state numbered around twenty thousand, with about 800 in Sacramento's new Chinatown on I street. Most of the rest were east of Sacramento, wearing their pigtails, pajamas, straw cone hats, and new American lace-up boots. They tramped over the Sierra Nevada foothills, busily turning them into a gigantic quarry. They brewed herbal remedies and cooked Chinese food over their campfires, carrying their herbs, sauces, sweet meats, and candied dishes wherever they went.

Despite their propensity for lucky strikes, the Chinese didn't overlook abandoned mines. They took dust and tailings and were happy for it. When they couldn't reach the ore, they built dams across rivers to get it. Although the Chinese were first welcomed to California as needed laborers, their unending zeal for work and their refusal to adopt American customs annoyed many whites. Americans were infuriated by the Chinese habit of hording gold and sending it back to China, instead of spending it locally. The Chinese were also thought to depress wages by working for low pay. It wasn't long before the Americans and the Chinese began to utterly misunderstand each other.

The Chinese knew by now that all the promises back in Hong Kong had been hollow. There was no big money; they were paid less, in fact, than white miners. There were no big houses, and whatever American hospitality they had known was waning. The Americans seemed wasteful, impatient, and inefficient. Many were drunkards. Still viewing their stay as temporary, the Chinese stuck together in Chinatowns—at Mokelumne Hill, Angels Camp, and on the desolate, windswept hillock of Chinese Camp.

A Chinatown was as big as a city block or as small as just a building, with services such as a laundry, a restaurant, a grocery, and a gambling saloon. Here the Chinese lived in cramped, squalid quarters. They subsisted on little more than rice and tea. Their stubbornly maintained culture became a focus of resentment and contempt. The Americans simply couldn't, and wouldn't, cope with the competition.

Gold, after all, is a one-time source of wealth. Once it's gone, it's gone for good. Whoever gets it first gets it for keeps. The Chinese had gone toe to toe, pick to pick, with the whites until the Americans' tolerance was at the breaking point. Politicians passed bills to tax the profits of foreign miners and to make the Chinese go home. As thousands of miners continued to stalk the golden veins, more than empty mines lay in their wake. Many Chinese lost their lives at the hands of angry American miners.

The Gold Mountain Gets a Railroad

After the Gold Rush, some Chinese left, but others stayed. Many went home and came back with their families. Although the gold had petered out, life in California was still better than life in Canton. The

Chinese consolidated their communities in San Francisco, Stockton, and Sacramento.

In 1864, the need for cheap labor arose again. The employer this time was Charles Crocker, one of the "Big Four" partners of the Central Pacific Railroad.

The new railroad heading east out of Sacramento was to be built quickly to meet the Union Pacific track heading west out of Omaha. With the supply of gold nearly exhausted, Chinese men were looking for work. Not many whites volunteered, so Crocker hired fifty Chinese laborers, who set up camp at the end of the track, ate a dinner of rice and dried squid, then woke up the next day and worked twelve hours.

By 1867, 14 thousand Chinese were chipping away at the granite heights of the Sierra Nevada. With picks and shovels, they worked through snowstorms, snow drifts, and Indian raids, and dangled over perilous precipices. Crews plunged into frozen gulches only to be recovered months later in the spring thaw, dead, with their shovels still gripped in their atrophied hands. An estimated one thousand Chinese were killed by ill-timed blasts of black powder, an unpredictable explosive used to cut through rock and hillsides.

The Chinese were angered when they found out they were being paid less than white railroad workers, but their strikes failed.

They were overlooked, too, when white laborers were fed beans, potatoes, and beef courtesy of the Central Pacific Railroad. The Chinese had to buy their own food—always the traditional rice, pork, chicken, seafood, salted cabbage, mushrooms, dried fruits, and vegetables—and, after a twelve-hour work day, cook it themselves.

Museums and history centers now honor the Chinese for their contribution to the settling of the American West. But the story of the Chinese immigrants had never been celebrated commercially—not until the Fat family created a restaurant to honor their history.

Frank Fat's Mountain of Gold

When Frank Fat came to America in 1919, the gold was gone. But in China the United States was still called the Gold Mountain. Sixteen-year-old Dong Sai-Fat, as he was then known, crossed the ocean, naively, to make a lot of money. He did, but not at first.

Sixty years after the original Chinese influx, immigrants faced new obstacles. Frank Fat spent a month on Angel Island, dodging questions about his American sponsor, until authorities finally let him onto the mainland.

Frank's "paper father"—whose claim to be a relative had probably cost Frank's grandfather a thousand dollars—took Frank to his uncle, who ran Hong King Lum restaurant in Sacramento's small Chinatown, on I Street. His uncle had a small house but no room for Frank to sleep. For a couple of months, Frank slept on the restaurant's cement steps.

During the next few years Frank held a string of jobs. He filled tonic bottles at a beauty salon, picked fruit in the Sacramento River delta, and worked in restaurants.

In a terrifying stint as dishwasher at Sacramento's exclusive Sutter Club, Frank came into contact with a violent chef. "The guy was so mean. I'm new. I don't speak. I don't do anything right. He throw the hot pan at me and hot water and soup went all over my face. I don't say anything, because I'm so nervous. Then, we had a big party, and I was supposed to go find a big platter. I was so scared, I dropped the platter. It broke in pieces all over the floor. I cut myself when I pick up the pieces." He stops to offer a view of the scar, still visible under the pad of his right thumb.

While his hand healed, he went to Chinese Church night school to learn English. Those lessons, plus about six years of schooling back in his village, are the sum of Frank Fat's formal education.

Frank went to Akron, Ohio, to work at a laundry begun by another cousin. "It was terrible, dirty. I said I don't think I can take that." He dismissed himself from the laundry business, and went to work in restaurants in Detroit and Chicago, ultimately as a waiter. "This give

5

me a chance to speak, to practice my English." He was never again without his Chinese-English dictionary.

None of Frank's jobs paid well, and one offered no wages at all, only tips. But Frank had learned that he could get by on very little money. "I don't spend a penny," he says. Today he still wears sweaters until they have holes in them.

In 1923 Frank Fat returned to China. A marriage had been arranged between Frank and Yee Lai-Ching, now called Mary. Frank stayed only until their first son, Wing, was born, then returned to America for more jobs as a busboy and waiter. He didn't see his family again for ten years.

Frank eventually returned to Hong Kong Lum in Sacramento, this time becoming a manager. One of the oldest Chinese restaurants in the city, Hong King Lum was in the 1930s one of Sacramento's ritziest banquet facilities. Frank's good nature made him popular there. With his genuine fondness for people, he began to develop durable friendships with the Sacramento politicians who came to wine and dine.

In 1936 Mary and Wing finally joined Frank in America. Then a dump of a restaurant went up for sale, at 806 L Street. Frank decided to buy it. He used all his savings, plus money given to him as a reward for honestly cashing a friend's winning lottery ticket and keeping the money safe until Frank at long last saw his friend again. In all, he bought the place for $2,000.

He named it Frank Fat's, and in 1939 he put his name up in front in gold letters. Despite what everyone said about the horrible location—that no one would even walk on L Street—Frank was positive that being two blocks from the Capitol counted for something.

He also knew he had the makings of a personable host, whose distinguished clientele at Hong King Lum might follow him to Frank Fat's. His smile, which crinkled the corners of his eyes, could melt away tension right through a three-piece suit. It was a smile that made people as intense as California politicians seek solace in his homey, dark restaurant. "I put my smiling face in an ad in the *Sacramento Bee*," Frank says, chuckling. "An old couple come in and pointed to me and said 'There he is! The man with the smiling face! That's why we come!'" (When Lina helped remodel the restaurant years later, Frank objected to placing a large, grinning Buddha in the restaurant and using it as a logo. "But it looks exactly like him, always smiling, tranquil," Lina protested. The Buddha is there to this day.)

Frank Fat's soon became known as "California's third house." For Republicans and Democrats alike, Frank's smiling presence was a relief at lunch, at dinner, and long into a wearying night. They'd huddle in a room upstairs. They'd meet at the bar. They came for the thirty-five-cent lunch. They came for the eighty-five-cent dinner. Frank's restaurant was the wheelingest, dealingest spot in all Sacramento. A long-time legislative worker was not stretching the truth when they told the press that Frank Fat's was where bills are born and passed.

Frank became a confidant to officials of both political parties. "I never butted in. I hear, but I never repeat, never talk. We are always friends, no matter who they are—we are friends." Among Frank's patrons in the early 1940s was Gov. Earl Warren, who many years later invited Frank to his chambers at the Supreme Court. Other governors, including Pat Brown, his son, Jerry, and Ronald Reagan were regulars at Frank Fat's, as well as Pete Wilson, *San Francisco Chronicle* columnist Herb Caen and assembly speaker Willie Brown.

The first menu was a hodgepodge of Chinese food and gooey American desserts. The Fat family became known for their cream pies as much as for their chow mein. Soon Frank created brandy-fried chicken, now a mainstay in Northern California Chinese restaurants (the recipe uses one-half of a chicken including the wings). And for the people who think no dinner complete without a piece of meat the size of a doormat, he developed New York Steak Frank-style, with onions and oyster sauce.

Before long Frank himself was a celebrity. He was especially appreciated, though, within Sacramento's Chinese community. A father of six, Frank became a benefactor of other young Chinese when the family established the Fat Foundation, which awards scholarships to Chinese-American students. As Frank's success continued, so did the family's loyalty to their fellow seekers of the Gold Mountain.

Another American Dream

Lina Yue's voyage to America was easier than that of her countrymen a century before. Except for all that on-board typing, it was a pleasant enough journey. She kept company with two friends she met on the boat. In dusty photographs the three of them are small and thin, naive, and unsophisticated, with crimped bangs and no makeup. Lina wore a Chinese *cheung sam*, a tight-fitting silk dress with slits to mid-thigh and a high Mandarin collar. "When I got to David Lipscomb College," she says, "they were very strict, and I was gently asked not to wear those dresses anymore."

She got only a quick view of San Francisco before leaving for Nashville, where despite her years of schooling in English she had trouble understanding the Tennessee drawl. She was one of only two Chinese students in the whole college.

Lina's diet abruptly went from Hong Kong stir-fry to Southern deep-fry. "I thought the Southern food was really bland. At first I didn't like grits and okra. I just couldn't eat that, or fried yellow squash." She liked country ham, but was unfamiliar with the Southern habit of dousing cream on everything from oysters to spinach. She took to cream readily in another form, though. "I loved banana splits. I ate them so much that I had to make myself stop, and for one year I avoided ice cream." The same thing happened with chocolate.

During holidays when the cafeteria was closed, Lina tried to cook for herself. She burned rice. "My friends said, 'How can you burn the rice, you're Chinese!' But I just couldn't do it right." Instead, she learned to make spaghetti sauce and Sloppy Joes.

After two years of pre-pharmacy courses Lina returned to San Francisco to get her doctorate at the University of California-San Francisco Medical Center. The money her father had deposited in the bank for her had dwindled, so she took a job as a live-in babysitter for the family of Dr. Alan Palmer, a fertility specialist, and his wife, Carlotta. "I was told I would be responsible for dusting, but I didn't know what dusting was," Lina laughs. "But I didn't mind." The family treated her as one of their own. To this day, Carlotta and Lina are like mother and daughter.

One evening she went to a student dance. "It was a very crowded dance, full of Chinese students," says Lina. "There was a young man crowning a queen, and he had a red face when he kissed her." I remember coming home thinking about him all the time. "Two weeks later, I glimpsed him on campus. A quarter went by, and our paths never crossed. One day, as I was leaving from eating lunch in the student union, the same man was coming in. And he talked to me. He said, 'My name is Ken Fat. What's yours?' Then he asked me to coffee, and a date! When I got home, I was jumping for joy."

"Ken Fat," she repeated later to the family she lived with. "Gee, what a name."

A year later Lina Yue married Ken Fat. She had no idea that she was marrying into a restaurant family whose customers huddled in a special room upstairs before retiring to their offices under the Capitol dome of the state of California. All Lina was thinking about was her new job at a Sacramento pharmacy, and having children. "I was not aware that the restaurant was a big deal. I was working most of the time, so I really didn't notice."

But being married to Ken Fat would, in time, bring her into close professional affiliation with her powerful father-in-law. She had become a member of a family whose livelihood would become her own for the next thirty years. She would soon stop using the doctorate of pharmacy degree she had so painstakingly earned.

Like her father-in-law, Lina Fat would become a Sacramento restaurateur of the highest rank.

Sloppy Jacques

After having children, Lina left her pharmacist's job to care for them while Ken worked as a dentist. J.C., Kevin, and Diana brought Lina into the realm of Cub Scouts and the PTA. Her only diversion was tennis, which she played every day for as long as possible. "I decided I was going to be an A-club player by the time I was thirty-five. I got a coach and took lessons. I really practiced, and three years later, I made it."

Actually, she was working on two goals at once. She had not forgotten her promise to become the best cook in the Fat family. She already owned hundreds of cookbooks. She had at hand the guiding words of Craig Claiborne, Michael Field, James Beard, Jacques Pepin, and other great chefs. She subscribed to *Bon Appetit* and *Gourmet*, *McCall's* and *Better Homes and Gardens*. As with everything else, she studied hard. And she experimented on a captive group of tasters—twenty-seven members of the Fat family.

"I actually learned Western cooking before I learned Chinese cooking." Lina says. Eventually, though, she decided to take on Chinese cuisine as well, and so she turned to Chan Wing, a famous Chinese chef and cookbook author. "I remembered what the food was supposed to taste like," says Lina. For centuries Chinese cooks had adhered to strict principles of flavor, appearance, use of heat, how food should be cut up, and balanced tastes. Lina was beginning to understand that she belonged in the kitchen and around food, but she needed the freedom to create.

When her daughter, Diana, was born, Lina decided to host the Red Egg party—the newborn's introduction to family and friends—instead of going to a banquet at a Chinese restaurant. Despite Lina'a heroic attempts, Diana's Red Egg party was a disaster. "It was in a small house. It was hot outside, and I filled a boat with ice and salads. The menu was ambitious, and I made these pastries with sour cream—four hundred of them, and I was rolling and rolling the dough on the worst possible day for it."

Still, she kept on cooking and throwing parties. Her entertaining repute spread throughout Sacramento. She signed up for cooking classes in Sacramento and San Francisco. Eventually, she became the cooking teacher.

Lina Designs a Restaurant

By the late 1960s, Frank Fat's was so successful that Frank decided to branch out. He had become fascinated with the history of his adopted hometown, Sacramento, and of the early Chinese immigrants to America. When a site became available in historic Old Sacramento, a slum area awaiting renovation, Frank applied to open a restaurant in a long, narrow storefront at 1015 Front Street. With this restaurant he wanted to commemorate the thousands of Chinese miners and railroad workers who had labored in California. He would call it China Camp.

At a redevelopment hearing, he was told that if he wanted to open a restaurant he should go to Chinatown. "I start fighting. I hire a lawyer. I don't want to be in Chinatown."

Old Sacramento, whose buildings were to be restored to their appearance between 1849 and 1870, would be the perfect setting for Frank's historic homage. But the family bogged down with details. How exactly should they carry out Frank's vision? They had to do something quickly, or the Redevelopment Agency would reclaim the site. They hadn't even thought about a menu.

"In the middle of the night, I got the idea for the menu for China Camp," Lina says, warming up to a favorite story. "Ken rolled over and didn't pay any attention." But Lina was wide awake, excited that she had found the concept to make China Camp a reality.

"I said to myself, why don't we use all the recipes from the family entertaining? We use broiling, the wok, the grill. We marinate with Chinese flavors. We eat Western food with Chinese treatments all the time."

She took the idea to her sister-in-law, Chee, who immediately added names to the dishes— Immigrant's Beef, Skinny Miner, Chicken Nuggets, Golden Spike Sandwich, Golden Hills Lobster, Claim Jumper's Beef.

It was a chance to combine cuisines more imaginatively than simply offering American desserts or a steak on the same menu as *moo goo gai pan*. Lina was dreaming up dishes that would mingle techniques, spices, cooking treatments, and presentations from both cultures, yet still appeal to Sacramento's rather hidebound dining clientele.

With a name, a theme, and a menu, all the family needed was an architect. Knowing that the most successful theme restaurant of the late 1960s and early 1970s was Victoria Station, Lina decided to find out who designed those boxcars into the biggest money-making dining experience of the times. With the help of her friend Maeley Tom, she found the architect, Don Wudtke, in San Francisco. His free-flowing ideas for trestles, tunnels, and mine shafts made Lina more excited. It took many family meetings and arguments, and much stalling, but finally the Fats were convinced.

As the drawings took shape, Lina realized that they were part of sputtering proceedings. No one was in charge of the China Camp project. Frank Fat was semiretired. Lina's dentist husband, Ken, was unavailable. Frank's youngest, Jerry Fat, was still in college. Tom Fat, now an attorney, lived in Los Angeles. Frank's two daughters, Jean Ann and Mable, either were not interested or living out of town.

Someone had to head up the kitchen and create a menu. As it turned out, Tom did return to Sacramento to head up China Camp, but it was Lina who developed the recipes and became the family's lifeline to the kitchen.

Lina worked out the recipes one by one and served them until all the family liked them, "and it was a big job to get the whole family to agree," Lina says. Instead of playing tennis, she helped lay out the kitchen. The next step was to train the cooks, who had been hired by her father-in-law and were all Chinese. It was Lina's job to tell them what to do. "I was very organized. I knew how much time the steps of each recipe took. It was clear in my mind who was supposed to do what, even what time to cut the beef, slice the meats for sandwiches, whip the cream, clean the barbecue." Lina's habit of following exacting pharmaceutical methods compelled her to a similar approach in the kitchen. "It was unheard of in cooking to be that detailed." She gave each cook a set of 5-by-7-inch flip cards, with drawings of the dishes and garnishes as well as recipes. Since this was the first open kitchen in Sacramento, she typed out rules of conduct: "DON'T smoke in the kitchen. DON'T talk loudly. DO wear a clean, white chef jacket."

What she didn't know was that Chinese cooks don't follow recipes. "They also had never learned to take direction, especially from a woman, and I had resistance from everyone."

Lina had no title. She was the daughter-in-law of Frank Fat, one of his sons' wives. The cook who gave her the most trouble was surprised to be greeted by Lina one day when he clocked in. She explained to him sternly that he must follow her instructions. "I asked him, 'Do you want to work here? Because, if not, there's the door.' He was shocked, and afterwards, he listened."

China Camp Opens

It took two years to complete China Camp, a multilevel restaurant with trestles over the booths, railroad ties for beams, and iron haulers and old mining tools for decoration. The front of the menu was a mock newspaper, titled the *Golden Hills News* in an Old West typeface. The menu ran imaginative accounts from the gold mines and gave a brief history of the Chinese laborers in America. Mining terms were defined and illustrated, lest anyone leave without knowing what it means to "pan out," "turn the river," or "ground-sluice."

The first new restaurant in the redevelopment area, China Camp opened to a huge crowd. Lina acted as expediter in the kitchen, calling the orders and garnishing the plates, as people spilled out from the bar. "We didn't expect to be that busy," Lina says. "The customers had patience to wait a long time for a table."

The customers reacted enthusiastically. For Sacramento in 1972, the menu was radically new. Dishes that were Chinese at heart were served American-style, with an entree, starch, and vegetable on the same plate. Western food was sparked with Chinese seasonings, just as in the Fat family's home kitchens. Beggar's Hen—simmered in a sauce flavored with twelve herbs and spices, chilled, then deep-fried to a crackling golden brown—was the most Chinese item on the menu. An offering called The Wok served heaps of stir-fried vegetables with almonds over rice. A Chinese oven provided the searing heat for glazing the menu's lamb and pork dishes. Chicken in a Clay Pot was Chinese comfort food. Drunk Steak was flamed with brandy. China Camp Omelette was scrambled up with Chinese barbecued pork. China Camp Broil combined an American-size serving of beef with a hint of oyster sauce. Immigrant Beef was marinated in soy, ginger, and garlic, and grilled. The names of the dishes by themselves appealed enormously to the clientele.

When she could see herself clear of the initial chaos, Lina created specials. "Lamb, which we always did shish-kebab style at home, but marinated in ginger, garlic, and wine, I did as a crown roast, and I used Western herbs—basil and tarragon, which are not found in the East. This was the first East-West dish I ever created."

There would be more. "Coming from Hong Kong, I was really privileged. I was exposed to the Western world and the Eastern world, and was able to taste both. I had the palate."

With China Camp striking it rich, Lina decided to go play some tennis. She handed over the restaurant to Tom Fat and his brother Jerry, who had just finished college. The restaurant continued in popularity, but behind the scenes something was missing.

Three months later, the brothers asked Lina to return to China Camp to direct the kitchen. This time, she stayed in the restaurant business for good.

Fat City

Two years later another burst of creativity from Frank Fat's dynasty targeted the dilapidated building next door to China Camp, on the corner of Front and J streets by the historic waterfront.

Built in 1849, it had been the first store established after the city of Sacramento was laid out. A photograph from Sacramento's archives shows "Henderson, Brown & Co.," a mercantile shop, anchoring a bustling street corner in 1890. During the restoration of Old Sacramento, the site came up for sale. It was just three standing walls—"a mess," as Lina describes it.

But China Camp's swarming clientele needed more space. The family bought the site, and restored the exterior to its original appearance. A fascination with Parisian bistros and fern bars, including Henry's Africa in San Francisco and Maxwell's Plum in New York City, led the family to a Gay Nineties theme. They planned a gathering spot with a simple bar menu to take up the overflow from China Camp. In the heart of restored Old Sacramento, the new place would appeal to locals and tourists alike.

In choosing a name, the family held a name contest during a Thanksgiving dinner. Matheau Palmer, the little boy Lina once babysat, came up with the double entendre based on the curious surname of the family patriarch. In Chinese, fat means "to prosper." They called the new place Fat City, a name that would signify prosperity to Chinese and Americans alike.

Then they broke through the wall between the two establishments and sectioned off private banquet rooms with beveled glass. They decorated with ferns, old Tiffany-style lamps, low-slung and tufted antique couches and chairs, tiny black and white floor tiles, and sparkling stained glass. The prized pieces were the colored glass dome in the ceiling and the famous Purple Lady, which won first prize in stained glass at the 1893 Chicago World's Fair.

They also hauled the legendary Pioneer Bar, circa 1876, complete with backing mirror and brass rail, from a soon-to-be condemned bar in Leadville, Colorado. It was stripped of a thick cinder-colored finish to reveal the mahogany wood, and the bar is now restored to its original condition.

Lina went to work on the menu, feeling her way through the countless culinary influences in her life and her conception of the mixed clientele Fat City would attract. Except for steamed fish, her new bistro menu was at first glance without a trace of Chinese influence. It did reflect Lina's personal fondness for French cooking; there was a quiche from her days as a home entertainer, tall, rich, and fluffy in a deep dish. There were Fresh Crab with Cream Sauce, French Onion Soup Gratinee, and Coquille St. Jacques. But there were also Italian fettuccine, and some all-American dishes, including gumbo (containing the once-dreaded okra, which Lina had grown to love), chili, Corned Beef Hash, Cherry Cheese Cake, and Deep Dish Apple Pie.

Having enjoyed espresso on a trip to Italy, Lina thought her customers would appreciate having it in Sacramento. She had the machine installed, and with it infused the restaurant with the telltale hissing of a cappuccino in progress. "We opened to diverse opinions. People expected a full-fledged menu, but it was really very eclectic, just a little bar menu," Lina says.

In a short time, though, the Fat City menu stood on its own, for the restaurant was no longer just an appendage to China Camp. Lina experimented with regional foods and flavor combinations now basic to "California cuisine." She added to the menu Smoked Salmon Taquitos, Southern Fried Chicken Strips, Spicy Beef Quesadilla, a club sandwich with sun-dried tomatoes, New Mexico Turkey and Chicken Sausage, and Angel Hair Pasta with Prosciutto and Olives. The quiche remained stubbornly in its place, however, a customer favorite to this day.

Although you wouldn't know it from a cursory glance at the menu, the Chinese influence is still strong at Fat City. Olallieberry Chicken Marinated in White Raspberry Dressing highlights a blackberry from the Mendocino area, but, in a nod to the Chinese preference for dark meat, uses just the leg. Linguine with Shrimp and Squid in Lobster-Flavored Sauce is based on the same flavor combination as another great Cantonese dishes.

Lina discovered it is difficult for a Chinese-born cook to stray far from the original course. "I remember one time in Hong Kong eating a soup with cabbage and beets and meat. I didn't know what it was, I just drank it, and it was great. Now I know that I was drinking borscht. I've had it many times in America. But I still remember the taste of the borscht in Hong Kong as being much better than any place else. The only thing I can think is that the cook must have been Chinese! He must have used some Chinese ingredients, because it was the best soup I have tasted."

No Women Allowed

At the urging of then-mayor Pete Wilson, China Camp and Fat City opened branches in San Diego in 1980. Besides running both restaurants in Sacramento, Lina served as consultant to the two Fat restaurants five hundred miles away.

Lina had taught herself to cook at home, and had learned restaurant cooking and managing simply by doing it. Over the years she had been given a number of titles—kitchen manager, food director, general manager. In 1978 she had been promoted to director of operations. Now, after ten years in the restaurant business, she wanted some formal training.

In 1984, Lina returned to Hong Kong for a culinary

awakening. With great chefs from China among the many new immigrants, Hong Kong was the perfect place to learn—"because of all the competition, and because Hong Kong was already getting big in the East-West mix," says Lina. She and the chef from Frank Fat's took daily private lessons from a master chef and teacher. But when she wanted to enter Chinese restaurant kitchens for firsthand experience, she couldn't. No women allowed, she was told. But Lina was undaunted: "We brought the chef back with us to cook at Frank Fat's for a year."

She took other learning vacations. On a trip to Switzerland, she fell in love with a strawberry tart. Upon her return she re-created it, but with a lighter pastry. "In France, I learned that French sauces are not so thick, that they are very clean and not at all heavy. And I also learned that my French onion soup is better than most in France!"

A six-week immersion course at the Culinary Institute of America (CIA) in Hyde Park, New York, gave Lina a perspective on her own abilities. "I wanted to know if I truly am a chef. I always thought it meant going to school, apprenticing when young. I wanted to see where I stood."

She took advanced classes in sauces, baking, and garnishes. Every Friday, she went to New York City to tour the best restaurants and meet their chefs. She discovered that her self-teaching, combined with her determination, had been as good as any schooling. The CIA put the polishing gloss on her handwork, but Lina truly already had cooking down cold. Now she felt she could use her foundation of knowledge to do just about anything she wanted.

She got the chance, when China Camp closed and was replaced in 1987 by a glittering phantasmagoric restaurant, California Fats.

California Fats

Whereas China Camp looked back, California Fats was all about the future. The world was merging into itself. After 140 years of immigration from the Orient, cuisines were colliding. The culinary possibilities were so exciting! Lina, now holding the title of executive chef, wanted an outlet for multinational experimentation. She wanted to mix Mexican herbs with Chinese spices. She wanted pizza fired in her Chinese ovens. She wanted Thai, Singaporian, Japanese, Malaysian, and Indian flavors in her food. And she wanted to pursue her own culinary fantasies without forsaking the past—or the customers.

Anthony Machado, a designer from Los Angeles, had worked with Lina and the family two years before in transforming Frank Fat's claustrophobic dining room into a gilded space with granite-topped tables and museum-quality antiques. He returned now to match the family's vision for California Fats with an equally fantastic decor. With Tom Fat again supporting the project, Machado worked like a geomancer, instilling Lina's philosophy into every detail.

At the back of the long, narrow space that once was China Camp, a three-story water sculpture, lit by a skylight and colored spotlights, sends sheets of water over a sheer granite wall punctuated by almond-shaped pieces of inlaid copper. The almond shape—an abstract Asian eye—is repeated in vibrant tones of gold, yellow, silver, green, and purple, in the carpet, in veiny art pieces over each booth, and in luminous metalloid sculptures on other walls. "The Chinese eye shape represents all immigrants' eyes on the future," Lina explains. "They're still looking for gold, looking for peace, looking for opportunity."

A Culinary Inventor

After twenty-two revisions, Lina brought out her California Fats menu. It featured "California-Pacific cuisine"—any country that touched the Pacific on either side was fair game. Most Asian countries and a number of regions within the United States were represented. Teaming up with chicken and beef could be nori from Japan; mint, scallion, lime, and peanuts from Thailand; pineapple from South Pacific islands; curries and hot chiles from Indonesia; ginger from any number of Asian countries.

An example of how Lina's concept works is Honey-glazed Duck, one of the first items on the California Fats menu, and probably there to stay. "It's very Californian, and also very Chinese," says Lina.

"Peking Duck is very traditional—the way you put the air under the duck skin and dry it out for three days before you cook it and put honey as a glaze on top is a very difficult Oriental technique.

"In China, we always serve Peking duck with plum sauce. I thought not too many people would like it here. It's quite sweet. Then I thought about one of my favorite dishes, duck l'orange. I love that one! But I didn't think orange sauce would go well with honey-glazing. I thought, too, that the color of orange sauce, yellow, wouldn't look good. But a very Californian sauce is with raspberries. If I could do a raspberry sauce, it would just be a touch of sweetness—not too sweet, not too sour—and the color would be pretty on the plate."

For Lina, creating a new dish starts with inspiration. She analyzes similar dishes in a way that's part science, part art. She imagines variations, and mentally tastes them. The skill in abstract thinking that got her through math in pharmacy school helps her decide which of numerous alternatives can best solve a particular problem.

Behind Lina's thinking is the instinct to balance what the Chinese know as the Five Flavors—sweet, salty, bitter, sour, and spicy. In a dish called the Hot Rock, chicken, beef, and shrimp arrive on a hexagonal platter skewered and ready for dipping in one of five sauces— sweet lime-ginger; hot chile oil; tangy tomato; salty soy; and a somewhat bitter peanut sauce. By itself this dish bridges the worlds of East and West by satisfying both Chinese standards of culinary propriety and the Western need for excitement and novelty.

Lina understands Western tastes. When she

wanted to introduce *wu gok*, stuffed and deep-fried taro root, as a new appetizer, she knew she had to get rid of the fat and the too-ethnic flavors inside. She thought that "it would be better if I put one piece of Chinese sausage inside. Then I thought about putting a piece of *gai lan* (Chinese broccoli) in there, and rolling it into a ball before deep-frying it. Outside it comes out crunchy, and inside are recognizable pieces of meat and vegetable. Besides, the taste is better—meat, vegetable, starch, just like in America!"

Lina knew, similarly, that pale, steamed chicken has little appeal to Western tastes. So she developed a recipe in which chicken is rolled, wrapped in plastic, briefly steamed, then *unwrapped* and grilled—an Eastern beginning with a Western ending. The steaming sets the shape, but the grilling brings out the flavor and makes the exterior brown and crunchy, the way Westerners prefer.

"When people say I am bastardizing Chinese food, I really don't see that. I am creating, following the basic rules of cooking. In Hong Kong, the better restaurants are all very innovative, all thinking about new things. Still, they don't vary the cooking techniques. Hong Kong didn't stay one of the most cosmopolitan cities from standing still. It's always nice to try something new, as long it's good, and not different for the sake of being different."

Lina intends to keep experimenting. She plans to add more Southwestern touches to the California Fats menu; she may hybridize Chinese tamales (*jeung*) and Mexican tamales, and substitute California short-grain rice for Chinese glutinous rice. She strongly believes that we won't see the end of blended cultures—and, hence, blended flavors and blended cuisines—any time soon. "Even automobiles use parts from all over the world. With cooking, it's the same thing."

Today Lina is, like her father-in-law before her, a Sacramento celebrity. In recognition of both her astute restaurateuring and her community service, she was named Restaurateur of the Year in 1987 by the Sacramento chapter of the California Restaurant Association.

Fat City continues to be Lina's personal melting pot. With its gumbo, fried chicken, and French abandon, it is probably the truest culinary expression of Lina's own life experiences.

California Fats is the result of Lina's prescient awareness of cascading cultures and her efforts to fuse them. With all its futuristic food and decor, you can still find reminders of the immigrants of 1849, if only in the railroad trestle still suspended over the booths, left over from China Camp. Their quiet spirit blends here with a feeling of American optimism and daring.

More apparent than the ghosts of the early Chinese immigrants, Frank Fat still watches over things, too. Now in his mid-eighties, he spends most afternoons in Lina's Old Sacramento restaurants, chatting with customers and occasionally serving up a free Frank Fat hamburger, just to witness the pleasure it brings.

Lina's mother could not have envisioned her daughter's journey from Hong Kong, where she never learned to cook, to her present position as matriarch of a Chinese restaurant dynasty in Sacramento.

Like the Chinese immigrants who scoured the golden hills of California a century before Lina came to America, and like her father-in-law, Frank Fat, Lina has faced challenges knowing at least one secret of life—that it is important to know when to let life lead you. When Lina let life take her into a restaurant kitchen, she unknowingly set forth on a path to her own joy, and to bringing joy to others.

It was a good thing she paid attention to all her trouble with a flourless cake.

Frank and Mary Fat at their wedding in China.

Frank Fat in Sacramento.

Frank Fat in China.

Frank and Mary Fat at the opening celebration of China Camp in Old Sacramento.

Lina in grade school.

Lina at a family dinner in Hong Kong.

Lina and the Sea Rangers.

Lina, her Aunt Lina, and
friend Doris at a yacht party.

Lina on a Harley Davidson.

Lina performing in the bicycle club.

Lina's 16th birthday party with her
father (center), Aunt Lina, and Uncle Wing.

*Lina in one of the party
dresses she designed.*

Lina in a bicycle club criterion.

Lina Fat, graduation time
from UCSF Medical center,
Dr. of Pharmacy degree.

Ken Fat, graduation time
from UCSF Medical Center,
Dr. of Dentistry.

Bar at California Fats Restaurant with sampan boat from Hong Kong (hanging top right).

California Fats Restaurant.

Fat City Bar and Café.

Lina and Chef Eric Beamesderfer in California Fat's kitchen.

Waterfall at California Fats Restaurant.

One of Anthony Machado's metal sculptures at California Fats Restaurant.

Appetizers

Chicken Satay with Spicy Peanut Sauce

Spicy Fried Squid with Tomato-Basil Sauce

Shrimp and Pork Wonton

Beef Siu Mai

Tequila Lime Beef with Green Onion Pancakes

Green Onion Pancakes

Sausage-Stuffed Mushrooms

Golden Nugget

Crispy Cheese Balls

Chilled Shrimp with Red Pepper Sauce

Smoked Salmon Taquitos

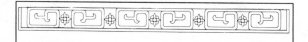

Chicken Satay with Spicy Peanut Sauce

Makes 4 to 6 appetizer servings

*3 skinless, boneless chicken breast halves
    (1 pound)*
16 bamboo skewers

Marinade
1/4 cup unsweetened coconut milk
1/4 cup half-and-half (light cream)
2 teaspoons curry powder
1 teaspoon each minced fresh ginger and garlic
1 teaspoon dry sherry or rice wine
1 teaspoon light (thin) soy sauce
1/4 teaspoon salt

Spicy Peanut Sauce
1/4 cup creamy peanut butter
1 tablespoon roasted, buttered diced almonds
1/4 cup unsweetened coconut milk
1/4 cup chicken broth
1/2 teaspoon liquid hot pepper seasoning
1 tablespoon lemon juice
1 teaspoon Worcestershire sauce
Pinch of crushed dried red chiles

On a food scouting trip to Southeast Asia I was intrigued with the little snacks sold in Singapore, Malaysia, and Thailand, and one of my favorites was satay—tiny skewers of grilled meat served with a creamy peanut dipping sauce. I couldn't wait to incorporate satay in California Fats' menu and now they are one of our most requested appetizers.

Remove the small muscle (fillet) from breast halves. With the flat side of a cleaver or mallet, lightly pound breast halves and fillets to 1/4 inch thick; cut into 2 1/2 by 1 inch strips. Using 1 strip of chicken for each skewer, weave skewers through chicken so meat lies flat. Place skewers in a pan.

In a bowl, whisk together marinade ingredients. Pour over chicken; turn to coat all sides. Cover and refrigerate 2 to 4 hours.

In a medium pan, whisk together sauce ingredients. Heat to simmering over low heat. Stirring occasionally, simmer, uncovered, for 10 minutes. Set sauce aside; reheat to serve. If sauce becomes too thick, stir in a little chicken broth.

Heat a griddle or electric frying pan with a nonstick finish to 400° F; grease lightly. Lift chicken from marinade, drain briefly, and place on hot griddle. Cook for 1 minute on each side or until outside of chicken is browned and center of chicken is opaque. When you turn chicken, add a few more drops oil to griddle, if needed, to prevent sticking. Arrange skewers on a platter. Serve sauce in a separate bowl for dipping.

Note: For a party presentation at home, I arrange the skewers clockwise on a platter lined with ti leaves, set the bowl of dipping sauce in the center, and garnish the platter with hibiscus or ginger blossoms.

Spicy Fried Squid with Tomato-Basil Sauce

Makes 4 to 6 appetizer servings

Tomato-Basil Sauce
1/4 cup sugar
1/4 cup lemon juice
1 tablespoon water
1/4 cup sliced mushrooms
1 small tomato, peeled, seeded, and chopped
1 tablespoon tomato juice
1/4 teaspoon each salt and pepper
2 teaspoons chopped fresh basil

1/2 cup all-purpose flour
1/2 cup cornstarch
2 teaspoons salt
1 tablespoon paprika
1 teaspoon white pepper
1 teaspoon cayenne
1 pound squid, cleaned, body sliced in 1/4-inch wide rings, tentacles whole
Vegetable oil for deep-frying

Squid has a chameleon-like character. You need to cook it very quickly or for a very long time. A mid-range cooking time results in tough meat. This California Fats' appetizer cooks tender inside, crisp and golden outside in 1 to 2 minutes. Be sure to shake off excess flour-cornstarch coating before adding squid to the hot oil. If left on, it sinks in the oil and eventually burns.

Combine sugar, lemon juice, and water in a medium pan. Stirring occasionally, bring to a boil over medium heat. Reduce heat to low and cook until syrup is slightly thickened. Add mushrooms, tomato, tomato juice, salt, pepper, and basil. Bring sauce to a boil; cook 1 or 2 minutes or until slightly thickened. Remove from heat.

In a pie pan, combine flour, cornstarch, salt, paprika, white pepper, and cayenne. Dredge squid in flour mixture, then place in a colander and shake to remove excess flour.

In a wok or deep heavy pan, pour oil to a depth of 2 inches. Heat oil to 375° F over medium-high heat. Cook squid, a portion at a time, until golden and crisp, 1 to 2 minutes. Remove with a slotted spoon and drain on paper towels. Serve the squid in a basket lined with a paper towel. Offer warm or room temperature sauce in a separate bowl for dipping.

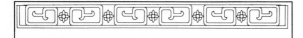

Shrimp and Pork Won Ton

Makes about 3 dozen, 4 to 6 appetizer servings

*1/2 pound medium raw shrimp, shelled, deveined,
    and coarsely chopped*
1/2 pound lean ground pork
1/2 cup water chestnuts, finely chopped
1 teapoon salt
1 teaspoon minced garlic
1/2 teaspoon minced fresh ginger
1/8 teaspoon white pepper
Dash of sesame oil
*About 3 dozen won ton wrappers (part of a
    1-pound package)*
Vegetable oil for deep-frying
Chinese hot mustard
Soy sauce

On this point, the savvy restaurateur and home cook agree: If a dish has a legion of admirers, don't change it. Fried won ton served at California Fats today tastes— deliciously— the same as the crisp won ton created by China Camp.

Combine shrimp, pork, water chestnuts, salt, pepper, ginger, garlic and sesame oil in a medium bowl; mix well.

To fill each won ton, place 1 teaspoon of filling in center of a wrapper (keep the remaining wrappers covered to prevent drying). Brush the edges of the wrapper lightly with water. Gather edges around filling and press together above filling to seal. Leave the ends loose; won ton should look like a pouch. Cover with a cloth while filling the remaining wrappers.

In a wok or deep heavy pan, pour oil to a depth of 2 inches. Heat oil to 375° F over medium-high heat. Cook 6 to 8 won ton at a time until golden and crisp, 2 to 3 minutes. Remove with a slotted spoon and drain on paper towels. Serve won ton with mustard and soy sauce for dipping.

Note: Most deep-fried foods taste best when freshly cooked, but won ton can be fried ahead and frozen. To reheat, arrange frozen won ton in a single layer in a shallow baking pan. Heat in a 350° F oven 10 to 12 minutes or until hot.

Beef Siu Mai

Makes about 2 dozen, 4 to 6 appetizer servings

1 pound lean ground beef
1 cup water chestnuts, finely chopped
1/4 cup finely chopped yellow onion
1/4 cup finely chopped green onions
1/4 cup oyster sauce
1 large egg white, lightly beaten
1 teaspoon cornstarch
1 teaspoon soy sauce
1/4 teaspoon white pepper
About 2 dozen siu mai wrappers (part of a
    1-pound package)
Soy sauce
Chinese chili sauce

*D*im sum—the time-honored midday fare of southern China—is composed of dozens of little savory dishes usually steamed or deep-fried. One of the tastiest steamed offerings is *siu mai*, a pouch-shaped dumpling open at the top. If you serve these as an appetizer at a stand-up affair, pass thick cocktail napkins with the soy and chili sauces. I prefer to serve them when guests can be seated and each has his or her own dipping sauce bowl and pair of chopsticks.

Combine beef, water chestnuts, yellow onion, green onions, oyster sauce, egg white, cornstarch, soy sauce, and white pepper in a bowl; mix well.

To fill each siu mai, place 1 teaspoon of filling in center of a wrapper (keep remaining wrappers covered to prevent drying). Use fingers to gather up and pleat the wrapper around the filling to form an open-topped pouch. Carefully squeeze the middle to give it a waist. Cover with a cloth while filling the remaining wrappers.

Place a steaming rack in a wok, add water to just below level of rack, and bring to a boil. Arrange half of the dumplings, without crowding, in a lightly greased 9-inch glass pie dish and set on rack. Cover and steam for 10 minutes. Serve siu mai with soy sauce or chili sauce for dipping. Steam the second portion of dumplings while you serve the first.

Note: The Chinese use many shapes of wrappers to make savory snacks. Won ton wrappers are thin and about 3 1/2 inches square; siu mai wrappers are thicker and round. Look for fresh wrappers in 1-pound packages in the produce section of supermarkets. If you don't use a whole package of wrappers one time, refrigerate extra wrappers for up to a week. Freeze for longer storage.

Tequila Lime Beef with Green Onion Pancakes

Makes 6 to 8 appetizer servings,
  4 to 6 entree servings

1 large flank steak (1 1/2 to 2 pounds)

Tequila Lime Marinade
2 tablespoons sugar
2 tablespoons each tequila and lime juice
1 1/2 tablespooons light (thin) soy sauce
1 tablespoon brandy
1 tablespoon each minced fresh ginger and garlic

Lime Ginger Sauce
1/4 cup sugar
1/4 cup each distilled white vinegar, dry white
  wine, and water
1 tablespoon lime juice
1 tablespoon minced green onion
2 teaspoons minced fresh ginger
1 teaspoon minced garlic
1 teaspoon sesame oil
1/2 teaspoon pepper
1/4 teaspoon crushed dried red chiles

About 2 tablespoons vegetable oil
1 medium onion, cut tip to tip in 1/4-inch slices
1 each red and green bell pepper, seeded and cut
  in 1/4-inch wide strips
16 Green Onion Pancakes (facing page)

When fajitas became the rage, I put a lot of thought into creating something more suitable for California Fats' menu. The result is a cross between fajitas and mu shu beef. It is not a collection of everything trendy folded in a wrapper—just a good combination of ingredients and seasonings that tastes light and interesting and is great fun to eat.

Cut flank steak in half lengthwise; cut crosswise in slanting slices 1/4 inch thick. Place meat in a sealable plastic bag. In a bowl, whisk together marinade ingredients. Pour marinade over meat and seal bag. Refrigerate for at least 2 hours; turn bag several times to distibute marinade.

Prepare the sauce: In a small pan combine sugar, vinegar, wine, and water. Stirring, cook over low heat until sugar dissolves. Remove pan from heat, add the remaining ingredients, and set aside.

Heat a wok or wide frying pan over high heat. Add 1 tablespoon of the oil, swirling to coat the sides. Add half of beef to pan and stir-fry until it is barely pink, about 2 minutes. Remove from pan. Stir-fry the remaining beef in another tablespoon of oil; remove from pan. Add onion and bell peppers to pan. Add a few more drops oil if pan appears dry. Stir-fry until peppers are tender, about 4 minutes. Return meat to pan and heat through.

Place meat on a warm platter. Place pancakes in a basket and lime ginger sauce in individual bowls for dipping. To eat, place a few slices meat and vegetables across center of each pancake on unbrowned side, and roll to enclose. Dip in lime ginger sauce and eat out of hand.

Green Onion Pancakes

Makes 32 pancakes

3 cups unsifted cake flour
1 teaspoon salt
About 3 tablespoons vegetable oil
1 cup boiling water
1/3 cup cold water
1/3 cup chopped green onions and tops

We serve these pancakes to enclose the stir-fried meat and vegetables for Tequila Lime Beef.

In a bowl, combine flour, salt, and 2 tablespoons of the oil. Mix in boiling water with a fork or chopsticks. Let dough rest for 5 minutes. Stir in cold water and gather dough into a ball. On a lightly floured board, knead dough 5 to 6 minutes or until smooth and satiny. Cover with a damp cloth and let rest for 10 minutes. Knead dough lightly, adding green onions as you knead.

Roll dough into a 16-inch long cylinder. Cut crosswise into 1-inch pieces and keep covered. To make pancakes, cut 1 piece of dough exactly in half. Roll each half into a ball, then flatten slightly into a pancake. Roll the pair of pancakes into 6-inch rounds. Brush oil lightly on top of 1 round and cover with the other round. Press the 2 rounds lightly but firmly together.

Place an ungreased wide frying pan with a nonstick finish over medium heat. Add 1 pair of pancakes and cook, turning once, until pancakes are blistered by air pockets and lightly browned, 1 to 2 minutes. (If overcooked, pancakes become brittle.) Remove from pan and stack on a plate while cooking the remaining pairs of pancakes.

Pancakes can be prepared 1 day in advance and stored in a plastic bag at cool room temperature. To reheat, wrap pancakes in a clean dish towel and steam in a bamboo steamer for 5 minutes. When ready to fill, peel off one pancake and put filling on unbrowned side.

Sausage-Stuffed Mushrooms

Makes 8 to 12 appetizer servings

24 large mushrooms
1 pound bulk pork sausage
1 cup coarsely chopped fresh spinach
1 teaspoon each minced onion and chives
1 tablespoon canned diced green chile
1 tablespoon heavy cream
1 teaspoon dry sherry
1 tablespoon dry bread crumbs
1 large egg, lightly beaten
1/2 teaspoon salt
1/8 teaspoon pepper
2 tablespoons butter, melted
1/2 cup shredded dry jack cheese

*T*his Fat City appetizer is easily duplicated at home. To get a head start for a party, stuff the mushrooms a day ahead, then pop them in the oven when guests arrive.

Rinse mushrooms and remove stems. Coarsely chop stems; set caps and stems aside.

Crumble sausage into a wide frying pan. Cook over medium heat, breaking up sausage with a fork, until lightly browned. Spoon off and discard all but 1 tablespoon of the drippings. Add spinach and cook for 2 minutes. Add mushroom stems, onion, chives, and green chile; mix well. Cook 2 more minutes or until spinach is wilted and pan juices have evaporated. Remove pan from heat and stir in cream and sherry. Add bread crumbs, egg, salt, and pepper; mix well.

Turn mushroom caps in butter to coat. Mound equal amounts of filling in each cap and press firmly in place. Sprinkle tops of fillings with cheese. Refrigerate, covered, until ready to serve.

Preheat oven to 375° F. Bake mushrooms for 15 minutes. Serve at once.

Note: Jack cheese comes in two forms, regular and dry. Aged for more than a year, dry jack is deliciously sweet and nutty and melts exceptionally well. We buy ours from Rumiano Cheese Co. in Willows, California.

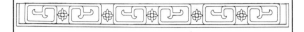

Golden Nugget

Makes 20 appetizers

1/4 cup uncooked California wild rice
1/4 cup uncooked California medium-grain rice
1 1/2 cups chicken broth
2 tablespoons golden raisins
2 tablespoons roasted, buttered diced almonds
1 tablespoon olive oil
1 tablespoon thinly sliced green onion (white part only)
1 teaspoon grated orange peel
1 tablespoon orange juice
1 teapoon chopped fresh mint or 1/2 teaspoon dried mint
1/2 teaspoon salt
1/8 teaspoon black pepper
20 marinated fried tofu pouches

New recipes are frequently "field tested" before they become a permanent part of our menus. I developed this appetizer originally to showcase California food products and served it at a shipboard reception before the Golden Bear sailed to Asia to promote Pacific Rim trade. Tasted and tested, this appetizer is now part of our catering menu. It's terrific tucked in an elegant box lunch or picnic basket.

In a 2-quart pan, wash both kinds of rice together until water runs clear; drain. Add chicken broth. Cover and bring to a boil; reduce heat and simmer 20 minutes or until all water is evaporated. Stir in raisins, almonds, olive oil, green onion, orange peel, orange juice, mint, salt, and pepper. Cover again and continue to cook over low heat for 5 minutes. Turn rice into a wide bowl and let cool completely.

Gently open each tofu bag. Without overstuffing, fill each bag with rice mixture; leave top open. Serve at room temperature.

Tofu Pouches

Japanese markets sell little pouches or bags of deep-fried tofu seasoned and ready to stuff. Look for them under the name *inari age* or *age tsuke*.

If you wish to make your own, cut 10 pieces deep-fried soy bean cake (*aburage*) in half crosswise and gently pull open the center of each to make a little bag. Simmer in water to cover for 20 minutes; drain. Return the bags to the pan and add 1 cup chicken broth, 2 tablespoons sugar, and 1 tablespoon soy sauce. Simmer, covered, 15 minutes; drain and let cool before stuffing.

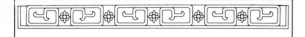

Crispy Cheese Balls

Makes 4 to 6 appetizer servings

4 tablespoons butter
1/4 cup all-purpose flour
1 1/2 cups milk
1/8 teaspoon each salt and white pepper
1/8 teaspoon ground nutmeg
1/2 teaspoon cayenne
3 cups (3/4 pound) shredded Swiss cheese
1 large egg yolk, lighlty beaten
1/4 cup canned diced green chile, drained and
    patted dry between paper towels
1 cup all-purpose flour
1 cup panko (coarse bread crumbs)
Egg wash: 1 large egg yolk lightly beaten with
    1 tablespoon water
Vegetable oil for deep-frying

*F*or years this was a popular bar appetizer at Fat City and we occasionally bring it back as a special. I love the contrast of texture: crunchy on the outside, creamy and soft within.

Melt butter in a 2-quart pan over medium heat. Add flour and cook, stirring, until roux (butter-flour mixture) is bubbly. Do not let flour brown. Using a whisk, blend in milk until smooth. Add salt, white pepper, nutmeg, and cayenne. Stirring continuously, cook over low heat for 10 minutes. Remove from heat and cool briefly. Stir in cheese until it melts. Stir in egg yolk and green chile.

Spread dough in a shallow baking pan. Cover and refrigerate until firm, at least 4 hours. With floured hands, and using 1 tablespoon of dough for each, roll dough into walnut-size balls. In a pie pan, combine flour and panko. Dip each ball in egg wash, then roll in flour mixture.

In a wok or deep heavy pan, pour oil to a depth of 2 inches. Heat oil to 375° F over medium-high heat. Cook cheese balls, a portion at a time, until golden brown, 1 to 2 minutes. Remove with a slotted spoon and drain on paper towels. Serve hot.

Note: Panko is the name of coarse bread crumbs, a Japanese product used to give deep-fried foods a crunchy coating. Buy panko in Asian markets or make your own this way. Remove crusts from firm-textured white bread. Whirl bread in a food processor to make even coarse crumbs. Spread crumbs in a shallow baking pan. Bake in a 325° F oven, stirring often, for 15 to 20 minutes or until crumbs are crisp and dry but not browned.

Chilled Shrimp with Red Pepper Sauce

Makes 4 to 6 appetizer servings

2 quarts water
2 tablespoons salt
1 bay leaf
1 small whole dried red chile
1 slice lemon
1 teaspoon dried dill weed
1 pound large raw shrimp with shells on

Red Pepper Sauce
1 large tomato
1 red bell pepper
4 whole cloves garlic, peeled
1/2 small slice French bread, crust removed
1 teaspoon olive oil
1/4 cup roasted, buttered diced almonds
1/2 teaspoon salt
1/8 teaspoon black pepper
1 teaspoon crushed dried red chiles (or to taste)
1/4 cup white wine vinegar
1/2 cup olive oil

*T*his appetizer goes so quickly at a party, you may want to pass the first round to be sure everyone gets at least one shrimp! The sauce is my version of romesco sauce, the dip served with cold shellfish at tapas bars in Spain. Unlike mayonnaise which is thickened with eggs, this sauce with a hint of smoky flavor is thickened with French bread and almonds.

In a large pot, combine water, salt, bay leaf, chile, lemon slice, and dill weed. Bring to a boil; cover and simmer 15 minutes. Add shrimp and simmer gently 3 to 5 minutes or until the shrimp turn pink. Drain, rinse with cold water, and drain again. Shell shrimp, leaving the tip of the tail shells on, and devein. Cover and refrigerate until icy cold.

To make the sauce, place whole tomato, bell pepper, and garlic in an ungreased pie pan. Bake in a 375°F oven for 30 minutes; turn vegetables and garlic over halfway through cooking. Let stand until cool, then peel tomato. Peel and seed bell pepper. In a small frying pan, toast bread in the 1 teaspoon oil until golden on each side. Cut bread in quarters.

Place tomato, bell pepper, garlic, bread, almonds, salt, pepper, crushed chiles, and wine vinegar in a blender. Smoothly puree. With motor running, slowly pour in the 1/2 cup oil in a thin stream. Pour sauce in a serving bowl.

To serve, arrange shrimp in a well-chilled or ice-filled container. Serve with red pepper sauce for dipping.

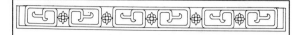

Smoked Salmon Tacquitos

Makes 12 tacos

Cilantro Marinade
1 tablespoon lime juice
1 1/2 teaspoons white wine vinegar
1 1/2 teaspoons water
1 1/2 teaspoons chopped cilantro (Chinese parsley)
1 shallot, minced
1/8 teaspoon each sugar and ground cumin
Pinch of salt
2 or 3 drops liquid hot pepper seasoning
1/4 cup vegetable oil

12 ounces smoked salmon
12 blue corn or regular corn tortillas, 6 inches in diameter
12 ounces cream cheese, softened

Condiments: *Salsa, sour cream, and lime wedges*

When you translate a recipe from restaurant service to home cooking, it's occasionally necessary to take shortcuts. Few of us have an assistant chef to help with last minute assembly, and when it's party time, guests take precedence over cooking chores.

At Fat City, we make tacquitos with small blue corn tortillas we order from a supplier. The tortillas are softened on an ungreased griddle, filled, and fried in deep fat until crisp. The presentation of the following recipe varies slightly: regular size tortillas are heated in the oven, not fried, and served like a soft taco.

Prepare the marinade: Combine all marinade ingredients except the oil in a medium bowl. Slowly whisk in oil. Cut salmon into 12 equal strips. Add to dressing and stir to coat. Cover and refrigerate for 8 hours.

Stack and wrap tortillas in foil. Warm in a 350° F oven 15 minutes or until heated through. To assemble each taco, spread 2 tablespoons cream cheese on each tortilla. Place a strip of salmon in the center. Drizzle a few drops of the marinade over the salmon. Roll tortilla into cone shape or fold in half and eat out of hand. Serve with condiments as desired.

Soups and Salads

Chicken-Vegetable Soup in Acorn Squash

Clam Chowder with Okra

French Onion Soup

Chicken Broth

Chilled Cucumber-Tomato Soup

Chilled Honeydew Soup

Tarragon Chicken Salad

Spicy Shrimp and Scallop Pasta Salad

Chinese Chicken Salad

Shrimp and Potato Salad

Summer Pasta Salad

Seafood Taco Salad

Fat's Caesar Salad

Spinach Salad with Roast Garlic Dressing

Green Bean Salad with Basil Vinaigrette

Tropical Fruit Tray with Poppy Seed Dressing

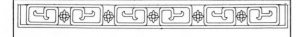

Chicken–Vegetable Soup in Acorn Squash

Makes 6 servings

Marinade
1 teaspoon light (thin) soy sauce
1 teaspoon dark (thick) soy sauce
1/4 teaspoon minced garlic
1/4 teaspoon minced fresh ginger
1/4 teaspoon white pepper

1/2 pound boneless, skinless chicken breast, cut
*   into thin strips*
6 dried Chinese black mushrooms
6 acorn (Danish) squash, about 1 pound each
4 cups chicken broth
1/4 cup matchstick pieces preserved turnip
1/4 cup thinly sliced carrot
1/4 cup thinly sliced celery
1/4 cup canned bamboo shoot strips
1 green onion and top, thinly sliced

As a child in Hong Kong, I loved the winter melon soup served at Chinese banquets. Juicy bits of chicken and vegetables bobbed in a sea of fragrant broth and the dragon carved in the pale green winter melon shell looked wild and fierce. When I designed the menu for California Fats, I wanted a similar soup, but one which could be made in individual portions. Acorn squash proved to be an ideal winter melon substitute. There's little chance of the sturdy shells collapsing from overcooking, and the golden flesh, scooped out with each spoonful of soup, gives extra richness and body to the broth.

Combine the marinade ingredients in a medium bowl. Add the chicken and stir to coat. Cover and refrigerate for at least 30 minutes.

Soak the mushrooms in warm water to cover for 30 minutes; drain. Cut off stems and thinly slice caps.

Rinse squash. Arrange whole squash so they will fit snugly in a baking pan. Bake, uncovered, in a 350° F oven for 30 minutes. Remove from oven and cool briefly. Using a grapefruit knife or paring knife, cut off a 3-inch cap from each squash. Scoop out and discard seeds and fibers; reserve caps and return squash to baking pan.

In a saucepan, bring chicken broth to a boil over medium heat. Stir in chicken, mushrooms, preserved turnip, carrot, celery, bamboo shoot, and green onion. Return broth to a boil; turn off heat. Dividing broth, chicken, and vegetables equally, ladle soup into each squash. Cover each squash with its cap. Cover pan snugly with foil. Return to oven and continue to bake 30 to 45 minutes or until squash caps are tender when pierced. Serve each squash in a wide shallow bowl.

Note: Preserved turnip is generally used as a cooking ingredient, but it can also be thinly sliced and eaten as you would a pickle. The gnarled vegetable is sold in plastic bags and cans. After opening, transfer to a jar and refrigerate for up to 6 months.

Soy Sauce

Chinese soy sauce comes in many varieties and grades. The two main types are light (thin) and dark (thick). Light soy, not to be confused with reduced-sodium soy, is light colored and a bit saltier than dark soy. Dark soy has a heavier consistency and sweeter flavor. Blending the two sauces in the soup (on the facing page) creates a balance of flavor neither sauce can give on its own. For most recipes in this book, unless directed otherwise, use a naturally fermented soy sauce. Chemically hydrolized soy sauces are not recommended.

Clam Chowder with Okra

Makes 4 to 6 servings

1 tablespoon olive oil or vegetable oil
4 stalks celery including leaves, diced
2 medium onions, diced
2 cloves garlic, minced
2 large bay leaves
1 1/2 teaspoons each dried thyme, rosemary,
    and basil leaves
1 1/2 teaspoons fennel seeds
2 cups diced thin-skinned potatoes
8 cups clam broth or chicken broth or
    4 cups of each
2 tablespoons clam base (optional)
1/4 cup tomato paste
1 1/2 cups chopped raw clams
1 cup (1/4 pound) okra, stems removed and cut
    into 1/8-inch rounds
2 medium tomatoes, peeled and diced
1/2 cup dry white wine
3/4 teaspoon black pepper
Salt

My version of Manhattan clam chowder has a southern accent—a carry-over from my days living in Tennessee. Like Creole cooking, it has a deep spicy flavor without being overly hot. For a light supper, serve it with French bread or home-baked wheat bread.

Heat oil in a 5-quart pan over medium heat. Add celery, onions, and garlic; cook until onions are lightly browned. Add bay leaves, thyme, rosemary, basil, fennel seeds, and potatoes. Cook for 1 minute. Add broth, clam base, and tomato paste. Bring to a boil; cover, reduce heat, and simmer until potatoes are tender when pierced, about 20 minutes. Add clams, okra, tomatoes, and wine. Simmer for 10 minutes. Add pepper and salt to taste. Discard bay leaves before serving.

French Onion Soup

Makes 6 servings

1/2 cup clarified butter, (page 109)
10 large (5 pounds) yellow onions, thinly sliced
1/4 cup all-purpose flour
4 cups chicken broth
4 cups beef broth
Herb bag contents: 1 sprig parsley, 1 bay leaf,
    1 clove crushed garlic, and 1/4 teaspoon
    dried thyme
1/2 cup dry sherry
Salt and pepper
6 slices French bread
2 tablespoons garlic butter, page 61
1/2 pound Swiss cheese, thinly sliced
1 cup grated Parmesan cheese

At Fat City you can order a small bowl or large crock of classic French onion soup. At home, I always serve a large portion in an individual casserole and call it the entree. Preceded by a crisp green salad and followed by a luscious dessert, such as Brandy Apple Tart (page 144), it becomes a fine menu for casual entertaining.

Melt butter in a 4-quart pan over medium heat. Add onions and cook, stirring occasionally, until soft and caramel-colored but not browned, 30 to 40 minutes. Stir in flour and cook for 2 minutes to brown lightly. Pour in about 1 cup of the broth, stirring to blend flour and broth. Add remaining broth.

Make herb bag by wrapping parsley, bay leaf, garlic, and thyme in a square of cheese cloth; tie bag closed with string. Drop bag into the soup. Bring to a boil; cover, reduce heat, and simmer for 30 minutes. Discard herb bag. Add sherry and salt and pepper to taste.

While soup is cooking, trim French bread to fit inside soup bowls. Spread each slice with garlic butter. Place bread on a rack set in a baking pan. Bake in a 300° F oven 15 to 20 minutes or until lightly toasted.

Ladle hot soup into six 1 1/2 to 2-cup ovenproof soup bowls. Float a piece of French bread on top. Cover bread with Swiss cheese slices. Sprinkle Parmesan cheese on top. Place bowls under the broiler about 4 inches from heat. Broil until cheese is lightly browned.

Note: Cooking the onions very slowly until they take on a rich caramel color is the secret of making good onion soup. If more convenient, you can make soup and toast the bread a day ahead. Reheat the soup slowly over medium-low heat before finishing the final assembly.

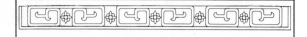

Chicken Broth

Makes 4 quarts

2 pounds raw chicken bones (necks, backs, or
* any other uncooked bones)*
1 pound pork bones with some meat on them
1/2 pound ham bone with some meat on it
Fresh and dried mushrooms stems (optional)
6 quarts water

Chicken broth is a staple ingredient in our cooking and you will find it called for in many recipes
throughout this book. This is the broth that we use.
Because I want a neutral broth that won't overpower
other flavors, I don't add onion and celery, but I add all
the fresh and dried mushroom stems we save from other
food preparation. The broth derives its flavor from
chicken and pork bones with no salt added. If, when
cooking, you use canned chicken broth instead of
homemade broth, dilute it with an equal amount of
water to make it less salty. When using salted canned
broth, it is imporant to taste a dish before adding the
suggested amount of salt.

Combine chicken bones, pork bones, ham bone,
mushrooms stems, and water in a large stock pot. Bring
to a boil, then reduce heat and simmer, uncovered, for 5
hours or until broth has reduced to 4 quarts. Skim and
discard sediment from broth frequently.

Line a colander with a double thickness of cheesecloth. Set colander in a large bowl. Pour broth through
colander; discard residue. Let broth cool; transfer to
pint or quart freezer containers and refrigerate overnight, then lift off and discard fat. Cover and refrigerate
or freeze.

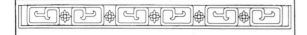

Chilled Cucumber–Tomato Soup

Makes 4 to 6 first-course servings

4 cups tomato juice
2 tablespoons tomato paste
6 tablespoons red wine vinegar
2 tablespoons olive oil
1 1/2 teaspoons chopped fresh basil
2 cloves garlic, minced
1/8 teaspoon cayenne
6 medium (1 1/2 pounds) tomatoes, peeled,
    seeded, and coarsely chopped
2 medium cucumbers, peeled, seeded, and
    coarsely chopped
1 large onion, coarsely chopped
1 each medium green and red bell pepper,
    seeded and cut in 1/4 inch dice
Salt
1 1/2 teaspoons chopped parsley
1 1/2 teaspoons chopped cilantro (Chinese
    parsley)
Sour cream

We feature this refreshing version of gazpacho on summer menus when sun-kissed tomatoes are juicy and sweet.

In a large bowl, whisk together tomato juice and tomato paste until smooth. Add vinegar, oil, basil, garlic, and cayenne and whisk until evenly blended. Stir in tomatoes, cucumbers, onion, and bell peppers. Add salt to taste. Cover and refrigerate until icy cold, at least 4 hours. Just before serving, stir in parsley and cilantro. Serve in chilled bowls. Garnish each serving with sour cream.

Note: If you prefer a smooth soup to sip from mugs or glass cups—an easy first course to serve before guests are seated—whirl the soup in the blender and strain before chilling.

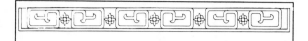

Chilled Honeydew Soup

Makes 6 to 8 first-course servings

3 honeydew melons
1 cup heavy cream
1/3 cup brandy
2 tablespoons chopped fresh mint
1/2 English cucumber or other
seedless cucumber
  Mint sprigs for garnish

Velvety in texture, soft apple green in color, this icy soup makes a picture-perfect opener to a warm weather brunch or luncheon. Use your nose to help you pick the ripest melons. A fully ripe honeydew melon will have a cream-colored rind and a pronounced honey aroma.

Cut melons in halves. Scoop out and discard seeds. With a spoon, scoop flesh from melons. Whirl in a food processor, a portion at a time, until smoothly pureed. You should have 5 cups. Pour into a bowl; stir in cream, brandy, and chopped mint. Cover and refrigerate until icy cold, at least 4 hours.

Serve soup in stemmed glasses or glass bowls. Peel cucumber and thinly slice. Float a few cucumber slices on each serving. Garnish with mint sprigs.

Note: For a cool presentation, I like to serve the soup in sugar-rimmed glasses. To prepare the glasses, dip the rim of each glass in lemon juice, then in granulated sugar. Pour the soup into the center of each glass so it does not moisten the frosted edge.

Tarragon Chicken Salad

Makes 6 servings

Glaze
3 tablespoons chopped fresh tarragon
1 1/2 tablespoons finely minced garlic
1 1/2 teaspoons honey
1 1/2 teaspoons salt
1/4 teaspoon black pepper

Tarragon Dressing
1/2 cup olive oil or vegetable oil
2 tablespoons raspberry vinegar
1 1/2 teaspoons glaze (above)
1/2 teaspoon water

*6 large chicken breast halves, skinned
   and boned*
1 cup raspberry vinegar
*3 cups mixed salad greens (butter lettuce, red
   leaf lettuce, and Belgian endive), rinsed
   and crisped*
1 cup fresh raspberries

*P*resentation ranks with flavor in our food so when I develop a new recipe, I file a sketch of the final assembly—the look of the dish—along with directions for cooking. Composed salads, like this one of fan-shaped chicken breasts, are visually exciting but not overly fussy.

Combine glaze ingredients in a small bowl; set aside.

Prepare the dressing: In a blender, blend oil, vinegar, 1 1/2 teaspoons of the glaze, and water until smooth; set aside.

Place chicken in a sealable plastic bag, add raspberry vinegar, and seal bag. Refrigerate for 8 hours or overnight; turn bag once to distribute marinade. Remove chicken from marinade and pat dry with paper towels. Spread a thin layer of glaze on all sides of breasts. Place chicken in a shallow baking pan. Bake in a preheated 350° F oven until chicken is no longer pink in center (cut to test), 15 to 18 minutes. Remove pan from oven, let chicken cool, then refrigerate for at least 1 hour.

Starting 1 inch from the top, cut each breast into 4 or 5 slices; leave slices attached at the top. Arrange salad greens on 6 serving plates. On each plate, fan a chicken breast on top of the greens; arrange raspberries over the uncut portions of chicken. Drizzle tarragon dressing over each salad.

Spicy Shrimp and Scallop Pasta Salad

Makes 6 servings

Thai Dressing
1/4 cup minced shallots
1 tablespoon minced fresh ginger
1 tablespoon chopped fresh basil
1 tablespoon chopped cilantro (Chinese parsley)
6 tablespoons lime juice
1/4 cup Thai fish sauce
1 tablespoon sugar
1/2 teaspoon salt
1/8 teaspoon crushed dried red chiles
1/2 cup vegetable oil

8 dried Chinese black mushrooms
2 cups chicken broth
1/2 pound medium raw shrimp, shelled and
    deveined
1/2 pound sea scallops, quartered
1 pound tri-colored spiral-shaped pasta
1/4 cup roasted peanuts, coarsely chopped
Cilantro (Chinese parsley) sprigs for garnish

*T*his pasta salad tastes especially fresh and bright. The secret is the Thai dressing which contrasts sweet, sour, salty, and spicy flavors.

Prepare the dressing: In a blender or food processor, whirl shallots, ginger, basil, cilantro, lime juice, fish sauce, sugar, salt, and chiles until smoothly blended. With motor running, add oil in a slow stream.

Soak the mushrooms in warm water to cover for 30 minutes; drain. Cut off stems and cut caps in quarters.

Heat chicken broth to simmering in a 2-quart pan. Add mushrooms, shrimp, and scallops. Simmer until shrimp turn pink and scallops are barely tender, 2 to 3 minutes. Drain; reserve poaching liquid for other uses. Place shrimp mixture in a bowl, add 1/2 cup of Thai dressing, and stir to coat. Refrigerate, covered, for at least 2 hours.

Cook pasta in a large kettle of boiling salted water according to package directions until barely tender to bite. Drain, rinse with cold water, and drain again. In a large bowl toss pasta with shrimp mixture. Add enough of the remaining dressing to coat pasta lightly; toss. Place in a wide shallow serving bowl, sprinkle with peanuts, and garnish with cilantro.

Note: In Thai cooking, fish sauce, also called nam pla, is used the way Chinese cooks use soy sauce. It is lighter in color and less salty than soy sauce, and despite its name, it does not taste fishy. Look for it in Asian markets.

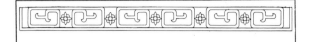

Chinese Chicken Salad

Makes 4 to 6 servings

Sweet and Sour Dressing
3/4 cup light (thin) soy sauce
1/2 cup cider vinegar
1/4 cup vegetable oil
1/4 cup sugar
1/2 teaspoon sesame oil

4 large chicken breasts halves
4 cups chicken broth
Vegetable oil for deep-fat frying
10 won ton skins, cut into 1/2-inch wide strips
1/2 cup sesame seeds
1 medium cucumber
1 cup sliced sweet pickled cucumber
*3 cups mixed salad greens (iceberg lettuce,
    butter lettuce, and hearts of romaine let-
    tuce), rinsed, crisped, and torn into
    bite-size pieces*
1/2 cup sliced almonds
*1/4 cup cilantro (Chinese parsley),
    coarsely chopped*
2 green onions and tops, thinly sliced
8 cherry tomatoes, halved

California Fats' signature Chinese chicken salad is ideal for weekend entertaining. Everything can be made ahead and assembled just before serving for a casual luncheon party. Look for jars of sliced sweet pickled cucumber in Asian markets.

Prepare the dressing: In a blender, blend soy sauce, vinegar, oil, sugar, and sesame oil.

Place chicken in a 2 to 3-quart pan with chicken broth. Bring to a boil, cover, and simmer until chicken is no longer pink in center (cut to test), 15 to 18 minutes. Remove chicken from broth and let cool. Strain broth and save for soup. Discard skin and bones; cut chicken into strips 1/4 inch by 2 inches. Refrigerate until needed.

Pour oil into a wok to a depth of 1 1/2 inches and heat to 350° F on a deep-frying thermometer. Add won ton strips in batches and fry until golden brown, about 1 minute. Remove with a slotted spoon and drain on paper towels.

Toast sesame seeds in a dry frying pan over medium heat, shaking pan frequently, until fragrant and golden, 2 to 3 minutes.

Just before serving, peel cucumber. Cut in half lengthwise and scoop out seeds; cut crosswise in 1/4 inch thick slices. Place cucumber in a large bowl with sweet pickled cucumber, chicken, and salad greens. Pour over enough of the dressing to coat salad lightly and toss. Garnish the top with almonds, cilantro, green onions, cherry tomatoes, sesame seeds, and won ton strips. Pass remaining dressing at the table.

Shrimp and Potato Salad

Makes 4 to 6 servings

Dressing
1/2 cup white wine vinegar
1 teaspoon celery seed
1 teaspoon salt
3/4 teaspoon sugar
Few drops liquid hot pepper seasoning
1 cup vegetable oil
2 tablespoons undrained capers and juice
2 teaspoons chopped onion

1 1/2 cups green beans cut in 1-inch pieces
6 medium (1 1/2 pounds) thin-skinned potatoes
6 cups mixed salad greens, rinsed, crisped, and
    torn into bite-size pieces
1 pound medium shelled cooked shrimp
1/2 cup pitted ripe olives
Freshly ground black pepper
3 tomatoes, cut in wedges
3 hard-cooked eggs, chopped

*U*sually served as a side dish, potato salad becomes a stunning entree when paired with green beans and shrimp. Just before serving, you toss the mixture with crisp greens and garnish with tomatoes, olives, and chopped egg.

Prepare the dressing: In a blender, blend wine vinegar, celery seed, salt, sugar, and hot pepper seasoning. With motor running, add oil in a slow stream. Stir in capers and juice and onion. Refrigerate until needed.

Blanch the beans in boiling water until crisp tender, 4 to 7 minutes. Drain and rinse in cold water to stop the cooking. Boil potatoes in their jackets until fork tender, 20 to 25 minutes. Drain and let cool. Peel potatoes and cut into 3/4 inch dice. In a medium bowl, toss beans, potatoes, and 1/2 cup of the dressing. Refrigerate, covered, for at least 2 hours.

To assemble salad, place beans and potatoes in a large bowl with salad greens, shrimp, and olives. Pour over another 1/2 cup dressing; toss lightly. Add black pepper to taste and toss. Arrange tomato wedges around edges of salad. Sprinkle chopped eggs on top of salad. Spoon the remaining dressing over the top.

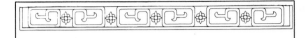

Summer Pasta Salad

Makes 6 servings

Garlic Vinaigrette
1/4 cup white wine vinegar
3 tablespoons chopped fresh basil
1 tablespoon minced garlic
2 teaspoons water
1 teaspoon sugar
1/2 teaspoon salt
1/4 teaspoon black pepper
1/4 teaspoon dry mustard
Juice of 1/2 lemon
3/4 cup olive oil

8 ounces rotelle or medium shell-shaped pasta
1/4 cup each thinly sliced green, red, and yellow
    bell pepper
1/2 cup Chinese pea pods, ends and strings
    removed, thinly sliced
1/2 cup asparagus tips
1/2 cup fresh basil, shredded
1/4 cup each grated Romano and
    Parmesan cheese
1/4 cup toasted pine nuts or sliced almonds

We make this color-splashed salad with bell peppers, Chinese pea pods, and asparagus, but you could use other vegetables such as fresh peas, yellow and green zucchini, and tomatoes. Blanch firm vegetables to intensify their color and flavor; use tomatoes raw, gently squeezing out the seeds before dicing the juicy pulp.

Prepare the dressing: In a food processor or blender, process vinegar, basil, garlic, water, sugar, salt, pepper, mustard, and lemon juice until basil is finely chopped. With motor running, add oil in a slow stream.

Cook pasta in a large kettle of boiling salted water according to package directions until barely tender to bite. Drain, rinse with cold water, and drain again. In a large bowl, toss pasta with half of the dressing. Refrigerate pasta and the remaining dressing until ready to serve.

Blanch bell peppers and pea pods in boiling salted water for 1 minute. Scoop out with a slotted spoon and rinse in cold water to stop the cooking. In the same water, blanch asparagus until tender but firm, 2 to 3 minutes. Drain and rinse with cold water. Refrigerate vegetables until chilled.

To assemble salad, add blanched vegetables, basil, the cheeses, and half of the pine nuts to pasta. Pour over the remaining dressing and toss until evenly coated. Divide salad onto 6 serving plates. Sprinkle the remaining pine nuts over the salads.

Seafood Taco Salad

Makes 4 servings

Lime Ginger Dressing
2 tablespoons lime juice
2 tablespoons white wine vinegar
1 tablespoon minced fresh ginger
1 tablespoon chopped parsley
1 tablespoon minced chives
1 teaspoon Dijon mustard
1/2 teaspoon Worcestershire sauce
1/2 teaspoon crushed dried red chiles
Pinch each of sugar, salt, and pepper
1 cup vegetable oil

Vegetable oil for deep-frying
4 flour tortillas, 8 inches in diameter
6 ounces medium raw shrimp, shelled and
    deveined
6 ounces sea scallops, quartered
6 ounces squid, cleaned, body sliced into 1/4
    inch wide rings
5 cups mixed salad greens (butter lettuce,
    romaine lettuce, head lettuce, and red leaf
    lettuce), rinsed, crisped, and thinly sliced
4 tablespoons each shredded jack cheese and
    Cheddar cheese

Garnishes: Diced tomato, diced avocado,
sour cream, sliced green onion, and pitted
ripe olives

*T*his is one of most popular salads served at Fat City. We make the tortilla shell from a 10-inch flour tortilla, mold it between two stainless steel strainers, and deep-fry it into a deep bowl shape for a salad for two. This technique calls for a lot of oil. At home, you can deep-fry two smaller tortillas with much less oil by using a wok. The curved sides of the wok help to shape the tortillas into shallow bowls.

Prepare the dressing: In a blender or food processor, whirl all ingredients except oil. With motor running, add oil in a slow steady stream. Refrigerate until needed.

Pour oil into wok to a depth of 1 inch. Place over medium-high heat until oil registers 360° F on deep-frying thermometer. Slide 1 tortilla into oil and press center into oil with tongs. While tortilla is still pliable, form a rim on it, using 2 sets of tongs to curl one edge up about 2 inches. Holding curled edge in place, submerge tortilla in oil until lightly browned. Rotate tortilla as needed so entire edge is curled and lightly browned. Remove from oil and drain on paper towels, cupped side down. Repeat with remaining tortillas.

In a 2-quart pan, heat 2 inches of salted water to simmering. Add shrimp; cook 1 minute. Add scallops and squid. Simmer 1 more minute; drain. Chill seafood.

To assemble salads, toss salad greens with half of the dressing. Divide greens evenly among tortilla shells. Toss seafood with the other half of the dressing. Arrange one-fourth of the seafood on one side of each layer of greens. Place cheeses opposite seafood. In center of each salad place a small mound of tomato and avocado. Top with sour cream and sprinkle with a few green onion slices. Garnish with olives and serve.

Fat's Caesar Salad

Makes 6 servings

Caesar Dressing
6 anchovy fillets, coarsely chopped
1 teaspoon minced garlic
1/3 cup lemon juice
1/3 cup grated Parmesan cheese
2 tablespoons plus 2 teaspoons sugar
1/2 teaspoon salt
1 cup olive oil

6 tablespoons garlic butter (page 61)
6 slices French bread, crusts removed , cut into
    1/2-inch cubes
6 hearts of romaine lettuce, rinsed, crisped,
    and broken into bite-size pieces
6 whole anchovy fillets (optional)

From its legendary origin in Tijuana, Caesar Salad has achieved classic status and, as might be expected, there are many variations. At Fat City we make Caesar dressing without egg and use aged Parmesan cheese to create an intensely flavored creamy emulsion.

Prepare the dressing: In a blender or food processor, whirl chopped anchovies, garlic, lemon juice, Parmesan cheese, sugar, and salt until smooth. With motor running, add oil in a slow stream.

Melt garlic butter in wide frying pan over low heat. Toss bread cubes in butter, then place in a shallow-rimmed baking pan. Bake in a 300° F oven, stirring several times to turn bread, 15 to 20 minutes or until croutons are golden brown. Let cool.

In a large bowl, toss lettuce and croutons with dressing. Transfer to serving plates. Sprinkle Parmesan cheese over each salad. Garnish each with an anchovy fillet, if desired, and serve.

Note: The most attractive greens to use in Caesar salad are hearts of romaine lettuce, but large leaves are fine to use if cut this way: with a knife, slit large romaine leaves through the center ribs. Cut each half crosswise in about 2 inch widths.

Spinach Salad with Roast Garlic Dressing

Makes 4 to 6 servings

Roast Garlic Dressing
2 1/2 tablespoons whole peeled garlic cloves
    (about 6 cloves)
1/2 cup olive oil
1/4 cup light corn syrup
2 1/2 tablespoons white wine vinegar
1/4 teaspoon salt
1/8 teaspoon lemon juice
Pinch each of white pepper, cayenne, and
    ground allspice

3 cups spinach leaves, stems removed, rinsed,
    crisped, and torn into bite-size pieces
1/4 cup sliced mushrooms
1 hard-cooked egg, chopped
1/4 cup diced red bell pepper
1/4 cup roasted, buttered diced almonds
1 tomato, diced
1/4 cup mixed salad sprouts
12 pitted ripe olives
1/4 cup thinly sliced green onions and tops

*T*his is a cool and crisp hot-weather favorite. Oven roasting mellows and tames the garlic in the dressing.

Prepare the dressing: Place garlic cloves in a small pie pan. Bake in a preheated 350° F oven, shaking pan once or twice to turn the garlic, 4 to 5 minutes or until garlic is golden brown and flavor mellows. In a blender, smoothly puree garlic with remaining dressing ingredients.

Place spinach in an even layer in a large serving bowl. On top of spinach make a layer of mushrooms, egg, bell pepper, almonds, tomato, and sprouts, arranged in separate, wedge-shaped sections. Place olives in the center. Sprinkle green onions over the top. Drizzle half of dressing over the salad. Pass the remaining dressing at the table.

Green Bean Salad with Basil Vinaigrette

Makes 4 servings

Basil Vinaigrette
1/4 cup fresh basil leaves
2 tablespoons dry white wine
2 1/2 tablespoons champagne vinegar
1 tablespoon lemon juice
1/2 teaspoon salt
1/4 teaspoon pepper
1/2 cup olive oil

3/4 pound green beans, ends trimmed, cut into
*   1/2-inch long pieces (3 cups)*
1 1/2 pounds tomatoes, peeled and cut into
*   3/8-inch dice (3 cups)*
4 ounces Muenster or jack cheese, cut into
*   thin strips*
Basil sprigs for garnish

Basil, green beans, and tomatoes are the essence of summer. For best flavor, don't refrigerate the tomatoes. Those that are ripe taste sweetest at room temperature. Those that are hard and pink will turn red, tender, and flavorful if left to ripen at room temperature for a couple of days.

Prepare the dressing: In a blender or food processor, whirl basil, wine, vinegar, lemon juice, salt, and pepper until basil is finely chopped. With motor running, add oil in a slow stream. Dressing should be thick and creamy.

Cook green beans in boiling salted water 4 to 6 minutes or until just barely tender. Drain, rinse with cold water to stop the cooking, and drain again. Chill until ready to use.

To serve, toss beans and tomatoes with dressing. Place on a serving platter. Sprinkle cheese on top. Garnish with basil leaves and serve.

Tropical Fruit Tray with Poppy Seed Dressing

Makes 8 servings

Poppy Seed Dressing
1/3 cup distilled white vinegar
1/3 cup sugar
3/4 teaspoon grated onion
3/4 teaspoon dry mustard
3/4 teaspoon salt
2/3 cup vegetable oil
1 tablespoon poppy seeds

16 pitted dried prunes
3 ounces Swiss cheese, cut into 16 cubes
1 mango, cut into crescents and peeled
1 papaya, seeded, peeled, and cut into crescents
1 small cantaloupe, seeded, peeled, and cut into crescents
2 cups seedless green grapes
2 cups black grapes
4 kiwifruit, peeled and thinly sliced
8 strawberries, hulled and cut in half
4 bananas
Mint sprigs for garnish

You could substitute other fruits or berries for this handsome fruit tray: the idea is to use the sweetest, ripest fruits in season. When you arrange the tray, alternate dark and light colors for a more lavish look.

Prepare the dressing: In a medium bowl whisk together vinegar, sugar, onion, mustard, and salt until sugar is dissolved. Add oil slowly, whisking continuously, until dressing is smooth and creamy. Fold in poppy seeds. Chill dressing for at least 1 hour.

Stuff each prune with a cube of cheese. Arrange prunes, mango, papaya, cantaloupe, grapes, kiwifruit, and strawberries on a large serving platter. Cover and chill up to 4 hours. To serve, peel bananas, cut in 1-inch diagonal slices, and arrange on fruit platter. Drizzle the dressing over the fruits or serve dressing in a separate bowl alongside. Garnish with mint.

Note: Sweet juicy mango flesh clings to the pit so you need a sharp paring knife to slice it neatly. To cut the fruit in crescents, score the skin lengthwise in 1/2 inch wide slices. Cut the slices from each side of the pit, then cut away the peel.

Pizza, Sandwiches, and Quiche

Pizza Dough

Roast Duck and Shiitake Mushroom Pizza

Smoked Salmon Pizza

Grilled Vegetable and Pesto Pizza

Pesto

Pepperoni and White Cheese Pizza

Fat City Sandwich

Roasted Red Pepper and Tomato Sandwich

Turkey Cracker Bread Pinwheels

Ham, Mushroom, and Onion Quiche

Spinach Quiche

Pizza Dough

Makes five 6-ounce portions. Each 6-ounce portion will make one 8-inch pizza for 1 individual serving or 2 to 4 appetizer servings

1/4 cup sugar
1 cup warm water (110 to 115° F)
1 package (1/4 ounce) active dry yeast
3 3/4 cups all-purpose flour
1 teaspoon salt
1 teaspoon cracked black pepper
1 teaspoon pressed garlic
2 tablespoons plus 1 tablespoon extra olive oil

*P*izza has taken a giant step forward at California Fats. Originally we baked pizza in our Chinese oven, but it has become such a popular menu item we installed a separate pizza oven. All of our pizzas are 8 inches—a good size for an individual serving. If you prefer to make larger pizza, use enough dough to fit your pan, about 12 ounces, and increase the toppings that follow accordingly.

In a small bowl, disssolve sugar in water. Sprinkle yeast over water and stir to dissolve. Let stand 5 to 10 minutes or until small bubbles form.

In a large mixing bowl, combine 3 1/2 cups flour, salt, and pepper. Make a well in the center of the flour and add garlic, yeast mixture, and 2 tablespoons of the oil. Mix ingredients with a wooden spoon until you have a ball of dough.

Flour a working surface and your hands with remaining flour. Knead dough 10 to 15 minutes or until smooth and elastic. Grease a large bowl with the 1 tablespoon oil. Shape dough into a ball and place it in the bowl; turn dough to coat all sides. Cover bowl with a dry cloth towel; let rise in a warm, draft-free place for 1 hour or until dough doubles in bulk.

Punch dough down and knead on a lightly floured board for 1 minute. Let dough rest for 10 minutes. Roll dough into a cylinder. Cut into 5 equal portions and shape each portion into a disc. Use immediately or wrap in plastic and refrigerate as long as overnight. If refrigerated, bring dough to room temperature and knead briefly before rolling out.

Note: To make dough in an electric mixer fitted with a dough hook, place dry ingredients in the mixer bowl and add garlic, yeast mixture, and oil. Knead the dough in the machine until it forms a smooth ball; place dough in a greased bowl, cover, and let rise.

Note: A very hot oven is essential to produce a crust that is crisp on the outside and chewy within. At home, you can get good results with a pizza stone which distributes the heat evenly. Preheat the stone when you preheat the oven; place pizza dough, without the pan, directly on the stone to bake.

Roast Duck and Shiitake Mushroom Pizza

Makes one 8-inch pizza

Olive oil
Flour
6 ounces Pizza Dough (page 54)
2 tablespoons hoisin sauce
2 tablespoons chicken broth
1/3 cup mixed shredded mild cheeses such as
  mozzarella and fontina
1/2 cup thinly sliced roast duck meat
1/4 cup thinly sliced shiitake mushrooms
1/4 cup thinly sliced green onions and tops

Not everyone is ambitious enough to roast duck just to make pizza, but if you make Roast Honey-glazed Duck (page 93) or buy a duck from a Chinese delicatessen, you'll have enough meat to give this a try. If you don't want duck, you can substitute chicken. It's not as interesting to my way of thinking, but good.

Preheat oven to 450° F. Lightly grease an 8-inch pizza pan with oil; dust with flour. Stretch or roll pizza dough into an 8-inch circle; turn up edges with your fingers to form a little rim. Place dough in pan; brush lightly with oil.

In a small bowl, whisk together hoisin sauce and chicken broth; brush over dough. In this order, top dough with cheeses, duck meat, mushrooms, and green onions. Bake for 15 to 20 minutes or until crust is golden brown. Slide pizza on a warm plate and cut into wedges.

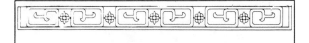

Smoked Salmon Pizza

Makes one 8-inch pizza

Olive oil
Flour
6 ounces Pizza Dough (page 54)
2 ounces cream cheese, thinly sliced
1 small tomato, thinly sliced
1/2 small red onion, thinly sliced
4 ounces lox or other cold-smoked salmon,
*   thinly sliced*
1/4 cup capers, drained

*T*here's no way to improve on the partnership of cream cheese and lox on a bagel—unless you bake it on pizza.

Preheat oven to 450° F. Lightly grease an 8-inch pizza pan with oil; dust with flour.

Stretch or roll pizza dough into an 8-inch circle; turn up edges with your fingers to form a little rim. Place dough in pan; brush lightly with oil. In this order, top dough with cream cheese, tomato slices, onion, and smoked salmon. Sprinkle capers over salmon. Bake for 15 to 20 minutes or until crust is golden brown. Slide pizza on a warm plate and cut into wedges.

Grilled Vegetable and Pesto Pizza

Makes one 8-inch pizza

Olive oil
Flour
6 ounces Pizza Dough (page 54)
1/4 cup Pesto (facing page)
1 baby Japanese eggplant, halved lengthwise
  and grilled or sauteed until barely tender
1 each small green and yellow zucchini, halved
  lengthwise and grilled or sauteed until
  barely tender
1/3 cup mixed shredded mild cheeses such as
  mozzarella and fontina
1/4 cup slivered sun-dried tomatoes marinated
  in oil, drained
1 tablespoon chopped fresh oregano or 1 tea-
  spoon dried oregano leaves
1 tablespoon chopped fresh basil or 1 teaspoon
  dried basil leaves

Summer's herbs and vegetables are the stars in this pizza. We use a light hand with cheese—enough to flavor the topping, but not make it overly rich.

Preheat oven to 450 F. Lightly grease an 8-inch pizza pan with oil; dust with flour.

Stretch or roll pizza dough into an 8-inch circle; turn up edges with your fingers to form a little rim. Place dough in pan; brush lightly with oil. Spread pesto over dough. Cut the grilled vegetables diagonally into 1/4 inch thick slices. In this order, top dough with cheeses, eggplant, zucchini, and sun-dried tomatoes. Sprinkle oregano and basil over the top. Bake for 15 to 20 minutes or until crust is golden brown. Slide pizza on a warm plate and cut into wedges.

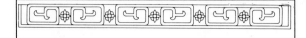

Pesto

Makes about 1 1/2 cups

3 tablespoons pine nuts
2 cups lightly packed fresh basil leaves, washed and dried
2 large cloves garlic
1/2 teaspoon salt
1/2 cup grated Parmesan cheese
1/2 cup grated Romano cheese
1/2 cup olive oil

A food processor makes this heady sauce with speed and ease.

Place nuts in a pie pan. Bake in a 350° F oven 10 to 12 minutes or until golden brown; stir nuts once or twice while toasting.

Place basil, nuts, garlic, and salt in a food processor. Process until basil is finely chopped. Add cheeses and process to mix. With motor running, pour oil slowly down feed tube. Use pesto at once. Or place in small jars, adding a thin layer of olive oil to each jar to keep pesto from darkening. Refrigerate for a week or freeze for longer storage.

Note: Versatile pesto is best known as a sauce for pasta, but it's delicious served atop hot cooked vegetables such as green beans, carrots, cauliflower, eggplant, potatoes, spinach, tomatoes, or zucchini. To give an instant Italian accent to soup, just stir in pesto to taste.

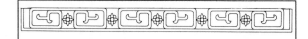

Pepperoni and White Cheese Pizza

Makes one 8-inch pizza

Olive oil
Flour
6 ounces Pizza Dough (page 54)
2 tablespoons tomato sauce
1/4 cup each shredded mozzarella and provolone cheese
1 Roma tomato, thinly sliced
1/4 each red and yellow bell pepper, thinly sliced and seeded
2 tablespoons thinly sliced green onion and top
3 ounces pepperoni sausage, thinly sliced

Red wine—zinfandel or a hearty country red—stands up to this full-flavored pizza.

Preheat oven to 450° F. Lightly grease an 8-inch pizza pan with oil; dust with flour.

Stretch or roll pizza dough into an 8-inch circle; turn up edges with your fingers to form a little rim. Place dough in pan; brush lightly with oil. In this order, top dough with tomato sauce, cheeses, tomato slices, bell peppers, green onion, and pepperoni. Bake for 15 to 20 minutes or until crust is golden brown. Slide pizza on a warm plate and cut into wedges.

Fat City Sandwich

Makes 6 sandwiches

Garlic Butter
1/4 cup garlic cloves
1 pound butter, cut in chunks
1/2 cup grated Parmesan cheese
1/4 cup chopped fresh parsley

12 slices French bread
1/3 cup mayonnaise
1/3 cup mustard
12 ounces thinly sliced cooked turkey breast
12 ounces thinly sliced pastrami
6 sandwich-size slices Swiss cheese
6 pieces of lettuce
1 medium tomato, cored and cut into 6 slices

In memory, I am a pharmacy student in San Francisco living with Dr. and Mrs. Alan Palmer and Mrs. Alan Palmer shows me how to toast a cheese sandwich on an electric griddle. What culinary magic—and so easy! Fat City Sandwich is an updated version of that sandwich, toasted to a golden brown in a zesty garlic butter.

Crush garlic with the flat side of a chef's knife to release skin; discard skin. With food processor motor running, drop garlic cloves down the feed tube and process until minced. Add butter, Parmesan cheese, and parsley; process until well blended. Reserve 3/4 cup of the butter for the sandwiches. Cover and refrigerate remaining garlic butter to use another time, up to 2 weeks.

Spread 1 side of all bread slices with garlic butter. On unbuttered sides, spread mayonnaise and mustard. Dividing the turkey, pastrami, cheese, lettuce, and tomato slices equally, place filling on 6 slices of bread; top with the remaining bread, buttered-side up. Grill sandwiches in a sandwich grill or toast in a heavy frying pan over medium heat, turning once, until sandwiches are golden brown. Cut each sandwich diagonally in half and serve.

Roasted Red Pepper and Tomato Sandwich

Makes 4 sandwiches

Sun-Dried Tomato Mayonnaise
1/4 cup (1/2 ounce or 8 halves)
    sun-dried tomatoes
2 cups mayonnaise

8 slices rye bread
1/4 cup sun-dried tomato mayonnaise
1/4 cup whipped cream cheese
1/4 cup mixed salad sprouts
1 cucumber, peeled and thinly sliced
1/2 cup roasted red bell pepper or
    canned pimiento
1 large tomato, cored and cut into 8 slices
4 pieces red leaf lettuce
1 dill pickle, thinly sliced

It takes 17 pounds of fresh tomatoes to make 1 pound of sun-dried tomatoes so you can expect an intensely rich tomato flavor from the dried product. In some recipes we use sun-dried tomatoes packed in olive oil. Here, sun-dried tomatoes are re-hydrated and pureed with mayonnaise, and plain ones packed without oil work best. You'll have leftover mayonnaise; try it on roast beef, club, and turkey sandwiches too.

Prepare the mayonnaise: In a small bowl, soak dried tomatoes in hot water to cover for 15 minutes; drain and allow tomatoes to stand for 30 minutes to become completely soft. Thinly slice tomatoes. In a bowl, stir together tomatoes and mayonnaise. Reserve 1/4 cup of mayonnaise for the sandwiches; cover and refrigerate the remaining mayonnaise to use another time, up to 2 weeks.

Spread 4 slices of bread with sun-dried tomato mayonnaise; spread the remaining 4 slices of bread with cream cheese. Dividing the sprouts, cucumber, bell pepper, tomato, lettuce, and dill pickle equally, place filling on bread spread with cream cheese. Top with the other 4 slices of bread, mayonnaise side down. Pressing lightly to hold filling in place, cut each sandwich in half diagonally and serve.

Turkey Cracker Bread Pinwheels

Makes 2 luncheon servings, 2 to 4
appetizer servings

1 Armenian cracker bread (14 inches in
diameter)
1 package (3 ounces) cream cheese, softened
1 tablespoon Dijon mustard
About 1 tablespoon heavy cream
1/4 cup roasted, buttered diced almonds
About 1 dozen large spinach leaves, stems
removed, leaves washed and dried
8 ounces thinly sliced cooked turkey breast
2 medium tomatoes, cored and very
thinly sliced

In 1983 when I demonstrated this sandwich on televison, Armenian cracker bread wasn't widely distributed, and viewers went to great effort to scout out a source. Today you can find cracker bread in supermarkets, delicatessens, and markets specializing in international foods. It makes a terrific wrapper for sandwiches-to-go.

Make them ahead for a box lunch or tailgate picnic; refrigerated, they stay fresh for several hours.

Soften cracker bread: Hold round of bread under a spray of cold water for about 10 seconds on each side or until well moistened. Place between clean damp tea towels. Let stand until soft and pliable, about 1 hour. The time depends on the freshness and thinness of the bread. Check often; if round still seems crisp in spots, sprinkle with more water.

In a bowl, beat cream cheese with mustard until smooth. Stir in cream. Add more cream, if necessary, so cheese mixture will spread easily. Uncover bread, leaving the bottom towel in place. Spread softened bread with cream cheese. Sprinkle nuts over cheese and press in lightly. Arrange spinach in a solid layer over cheese; cover spinach with turkey. Cover turkey with tomato slices. Using the towel to help you roll, roll bread jelly-roll style. Cover with plastic wrap or damp paper towels and refrigerate up to 2 to 4 hours. To serve, trim ends with a serrated knife, then cut roll into 10 to 12 slices.

Ham, Mushroom, and Onion Quiche

Makes 6 to 8 servings

Pastry
2 cups all-purpose flour
1 teaspoon salt
1/2 cup firm cold butter
1/2 cup firm cold margarine
1/3 cup ice water

2 cups diced cooked honey-cured ham
2 tablespoons vegetable oil
2 cups diced onions
2 cups sliced mushrooms
4 large eggs
4 large egg yolks
3 cups heavy cream
1 teaspoon salt
1/2 teaspoon white pepper
3/4 cup shredded Swiss cheese
3/4 cup grated Parmesan cheese

*T*his quiche wins the award as the most requested recipe. It was a winner in the early 70's when I cooked just for family and friends, and its permanent place on Fat City's menu has only widened its circle of fans.

Make the crust: Place flour and salt in a food processor fitted with a metal blade. Process 2 seconds. Cut butter and margarine into 1/2-inch chunks and distribute over the flour. Process until fat particles look like small peas, 6 to 8 seconds. With motor running, add ice water through the feed tube. Process just until dough forms a ball.

Shape dough into a 4-inch round; dust with flour. Wrap dough tightly in plastic wrap. Refrigerate for at least 1 hour. On a lightly floured board, roll out dough until it is 1/4 inch thick and makes a circle 16 inches in diameter. Ease dough into a greased 10 inch wide by 2 1/2 inch deep flan pan with a false bottom. Fold edges under and press against rim of pan. Prick bottom of pastry in several places with a fork. Place pastry-lined pan in freezer for 30 minutes.

Preheat oven to 350° F. Cover bottom of frozen pastry with foil; place 1/2 inch of dried beans over foil. Bake in preheated oven for 20 minutes. Remove pastry from oven; lift off foil and beans. Reduce oven temperature to 250° F.

In a wide frying pan with a non-stick finish, cook ham over medium heat until lightly browned and all liquid has evaporated. Remove from pan. In the same pan, cook onion in 1 tablespoon of the oil until soft. Add to ham. In the same pan, cook mushrooms in the remaining tablespoon oil until they release their liquid and all pan juice have evaporated. Add to ham; mix lightly.

In a large bowl, beat eggs and egg yolks with a whisk until evenly blended. Whisk in cream, salt, and pepper. Stir in cheeses.

Spread ham mixture over bottom of pre-baked pastry shell. Ladle egg-cheese mixture over the ham. Bake in 250° oven for 1 to 1 1/2 hours or until a knife inserted in center comes out clean. Let stand for 10 minutes before cutting.

Spinach Quiche

Makes 6 to 8 servings

Prebaked pastry shell (page 64)
2 bunches (1 1/2 pounds) spinach
4 large eggs
4 large egg yolks
3 cups heavy cream
2 tablespoons Dijon mustard
1 teaspoon ground nutmeg
1 teaspoon salt
1/2 teaspoon white pepper
3/4 cup shredded Swiss cheese
3/4 cup grated Parmesan cheese

*T*his is as smooth and impressively tall as the previous quiche, but it is made without meat.

Make pastry, line 10-inch wide by 2 1/2 inch deep flan pan, and prebake pastry as directed for Ham, Mushroom, and Onion Quiche. Set oven temperature at 250° F.

Remove spinach stems; wash and drain leaves. Finely chop leaves in a food processor or with a heavy chef's knife. Place spinach in a clean tea towel; wring towel to squeeze spinach dry.

In a large bowl, beat eggs and egg yolks with a whisk until evenly blended. Whisk in cream, mustard, nutmeg, salt, and pepper. Stir in cheeses; fold in spinach until evenly mixed. Ladle filling in to prebaked pastry shell. Bake in 250° oven for 1 to 1 1/2 hours or until a knife inserted in center comes out clean. Let stand for 10 minutes before cutting.

Noodles and Pasta

Barbecued Pork Lo Mein

Fat's Chicken Chow Mein

Yak-A-Mein

Honey Roast Duck with Spinach Noodles

Fettuccine with Chicken in Marsala Wine Sauce

Angel Hair Pasta with Smoked Mussels

Fettuccine with Shrimp and Squid

Ziti with Fresh Tomato and Olives

Red Pepper Fettuccine and Corn in Achiote Tomato Sauce

Achiote Tomato Sauce

Vegetable Lasagne

Barbecued Pork Lo Mein

Makes 4 servings

1 cup chicken broth
1/4 cup oyster sauce
1 tablespoon sesame oil
1 teaspoon Thai chili paste
1/2 teaspoon white pepper
1 tablespoon sesame seeds
8 ounces Chinese egg noodles
2 tablespoons vegetable oil
2 teaspoons minced fresh ginger
1/2 cup thinly sliced carrot
1/2 cup thinly sliced leek (white part only)
1/4 cup thinly sliced red bell pepper
1/2 cup beans sprouts
2 green onions and tops, thinly sliced
8 ounces Barbecued Pork Loin (page 123) or
    sugar-cured baked ham, fat trimmed,
    thinly sliced
Cilantro (Chinese parsley) sprigs for garnish

*L*o mein refers to a style of noodle preparation in which noodles are lightly tossed and coated with sauce. The more embellishments you incorporate in the sauce, the more flavorful the dish. At California Fats, we add vegetables and slices of our barbecued pork loin. If your prefer, you can substitute purchased Chinese barbecued pork for the pork loin.

In a small bowl, combine chicken broth, oyster sauce, sesame oil, chili paste, and white pepper; set aside. Toast sesame seeds in a dry frying pan over medium heat, shaking pan frequently, until fragrant and golden, 2 to 3 minutes.

Cook noodles in a large kettle of boiling water according to package directions until barely tender to bite. Drain.

While noodles are cooking, heat a wok over high heat. Add vegetable oil. When oil is hot, add ginger, carrot, leek, bell pepper, bean sprouts, and green onions. Stir-fry until vegetables are crisp-tender, about 2 minutes. Add chicken broth mixture and pork. Cook until sauce is heated through. Add hot noodles to pan and toss lightly until evenly mixed. Place on a warm platter. Sprinkle sesame seeds over the top and garnish with cilantro.

Note: Asian markets sell an amazing array of pastes made from chiles, soybeans, and salt; some contain a large amount of garlic. I like the fiery heat of Thai chili paste, but you can use one of the Chinese chili pastes if you prefer. If you use searingly hot chili paste, adjust the recipe amount according to your taste. After opening, store chili paste in the refrigerator.

Fat's Chicken Chow Mein

Makes 4 servings

4 dried Chinese black mushrooms
1/2 cup warm water
1/4 cup oyster sauce
1/2 cup chicken broth
2 tablespoons dry white wine
1 teaspoon sesame oil
8 ounces Chinese egg noodles
4 tablespoons vegetable oil
1 tablespoon minced fresh ginger
4 chicken breast halves, skinned, boned, and
    thinly sliced
1 medium carrot, thinly sliced, blanched for
    1 minute, drained
1 cup Chinese pea pods, ends and strings
    removed, thinly sliced
1 cup bean sprouts
4 green onions and tops, thinly sliced

*P*an-frying noodles is the technique you use to make chow mein. Golden and crispy on the outside, soft within, the noodles soak up the richly flavored sauce during the final tossing.

Soak mushrooms in the 1/2 cup warm water for 30 minutes. Pour off most of soaking liquid into a medium bowl and reserve; discard sandy portion at bottom of soaking water. Cut off mushroom stems; thinly slice caps. Add oyster sauce, chicken broth, wine, and sesame oil to mushroom soaking liquid.

Cook noodles in a large kettle of boiling water according to package directions until barely tender to bite. Drain, rinse with cold water, and drain again. Place a wide frying pan with a non-stick finish over medium-high heat until hot. Add 2 tablespoons of the oil. Spread noodles in an even layer and cook, turning once, until golden brown outside but still soft within. Remove pan from heat.

Heat a wok over high heat. Add the remaining 2 tablespoons oil. When oil is hot, add ginger and chicken. Stir-fry for 1 minute. Add mushrooms, carrot, pea pods, bean sprouts, and green onions. Stir-fry for 1 minute. Add oyster sauce mixture. Separate noodles and toss in pan. Stir and toss until chow mein is well mixed and heated through.

Yak-A-Mein

Makes 6 servings

8 dried Chinese black mushrooms
1 cup warm water
12 cups chicken broth (page 40)
1/2 cup light (thin) soy sauce
1 cup oyster sauce
2 or 3 baby bok choy or 1/2 pound regular bok
    choy
8 ounces Chinese egg noodles or linguine
1/2 pound medium raw shrimp, shelled and
    deveined
1 large chicken breast half, skinned, boned, and
    thinly sliced
1/2 cup sliced water chestnuts
1 medium carrot, thinly sliced
1/2 cup Chinese pea pods, ends and strings
    removed
Salt and pepper
1/4 pound Barbecued Pork Loin (page 123) or
    sugar-cured baked ham, fat trimmed and
    thinly sliced

Frank Fat, my father-in-law, named this dish yak-a-mein because it resembles the basic bowl of noodles eaten throughout China. In Chinese, mein means noodles and yak indicates one bowl. While this is not a regular item on the menu at California Fats, we make it for customers who relish old-fashioned comfort food. For the desireable clear light flavor, it is important to use freshly made unsalted chicken broth in this recipe .

Soak mushrooms in the 1 cup warm water for 30 minutes. Pour off most of soaking water into a small bowl and set aside; discard sandy portion at bottom of soaking water. Cut off mushrooms stems and thinly slice caps.

In a 5-quart pan, combine chicken broth, soy sauce, oyster sauce, and mushroom soaking liquid. Bring to a boil; reduce heat and simmer for 5 minutes. Cut baby boy choy in quarters lengthwise. If using regular bok choy, slice stalks and coarsely shred leaves.

Cook noodles in a large kettle of boiling water according to package directions until barely tender to bite. Drain, rinse with cold water, and drain again. Divide noodles among 6 large bowls.

Add bok choy, shrimp, chicken, water chestnuts, and carrot to simmering chicken broth. Stir several times, then simmer until chicken is opaque and vegetables are just tender, 2 to 3 minutes. Add pea pods and salt and pepper to taste; cook 30 seconds. Ladle broth and vegetables into each bowl of noodles. Top each serving with a few slices of barbecued pork.

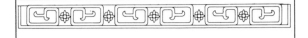

Honey Roast Duck with Spinach Noodles

Makes 4 servings

1/2 roast honey-glazed duck (page 93)
1 orange
1/2 cup chicken broth
1/4 cup oyster sauce
1 teaspoon sesame oil
8 ounces spinach fettuccine
2 tablespoons vegetable oil
1/2 cup thinly sliced carrot, blanched for 1
　　minute, drained
2 green onions and tops, thinly sliced
1/4 cup sliced sweet pickled red ginger
Salt and pepper
Cilantro (Chinese parsley) sprigs for garnish

We roast ducks daily in our Chinese oven at California Fats so we have a continual supply of crisp-skinned duck for this special pasta. As a shortcut, you can use Cantonese roast duck purchased from a Chinese deli.

Cut duck breast from the carcass in one piece. Remove skin and scrape off fat. Cut breast and skin crosswise in very thin slices. Remove remaining meat from carcass; cut into shreds, discarding fat as you cut. With a paring knife, cut peel and white pith from orange. Cut toward center of orange on one side of white membrane and slide fruit segment off. Repeat, removing all segments. In a small bowl, combine chicken broth, oyster sauce, and sesame oil.

Cook pasta in a large kettle of boiling salted water according to package directions until barely tender to bite. Drain.

While pasta is cooking, place a wok or wide frying pan over medium heat. Add vegetable oil. When oil is hot, add carrot and green onions. Stir-fry for 1 minute. Add duck meat and pickled ginger. Cook for 1 minute. Add chicken broth mixture and orange segments. Heat sauce to simmering. Add salt and pepper to taste.

Place pasta in a warm serving bowl, pour sauce over pasta, and toss. Garnish with cilantro.

Note: Look for Chinese sweet pickled ginger in Asian markets. The color is bright red and the ginger is cut in tiny julienne strips.

Fettuccine with Chicken in Marsala Wine Sauce

Makes 6 servings

8 chicken breast halves, skinned, boned, and
*   cut into thin strips*
All-purpose flour
2 tablespoons olive oil
Salt and pepper
1 medium onion, diced
1 cup (3 ounces) sliced mushrooms
1 teaspoon minced garlic
1 teaspoon minced shallot
1/2 cup dry Marsala wine
1 cups beef broth
1 large tomato, peeled and diced
3 green onions and tops, chopped
1 pound fettuccine

*L*aced with slices of chicken, onion, and mushrooms, this unthickened sauce lightly coats the pasta. The flavor is intensified with Marsala, a fortified Sicilian wine used in Italian cooking. Check the label on the bottle. You need dry Marsala wine, not sweet.

Dust chicken with flour. Heat oil in a wide frying pan over medium-high heat. Add chicken and cook until golden brown, 3 to 4 minutes total. Add salt and pepper to taste. Drain excess pan drippings. Add onion and mushrooms and cook, stirring occasionally, until onion is soft, about 4 minutes. Add garlic and shallot and cook 1 minute. Add wine, broth, tomato, and green onions. Heat through.

Meanwhile, cook pasta in a large kettle of boiling salted water according to package directions until barely tender to bite. Drain pasta and place in a warm serving bowl. Pour sauce over pasta, toss lightly, and serve.

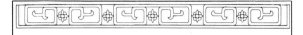

Angel Hair Pasta with Smoked Mussels

Makes 4 servings

8 ounces angel hair pasta
1/4 cup chicken broth
1/4 cup oyster sauce
1 teaspoon sesame oil
1/4 cup olive oil or vegetable oil
1/2 cup thinly sliced onion
1/4 cup thinly sliced green zucchini
1/4 cup thinly sliced yellow squash
1/4 cup thinly sliced carrot, blanched for
    1 minute, drained
1/4 cup sun-dried tomatoes marinated in
    olive oil, thinly sliced
24 pieces smoked mussels
2 greens onions and tops, slivered

*S*ome new recipe ideas take form when we come across an interesting product. One of our purveyors brought samples of smoked mussels and their flavor seemed like a good match for sun-dried tomatoes as a sauce for pasta. I added zucchini and carrot for texture and oyster sauce to echo the smoked seafood flavor. Smoked mussels are packed without oil and sold frozen in gourmet grocery stores.

Cook pasta in a large kettle of boiling salted water according to package directions until barely tender to bite. Drain.

While pasta is cooking, whisk together chicken broth, oyster sauce, and sesame oil in a small bowl. Heat olive oil in a wok or wide frying pan over medium heat. Add onion, green and yellow zucchini, carrot, and sun-dried tomatoes. Cook for 2 minutes or until vegetables are just tender. Add chicken broth mixture and mussels. Heat through. Add hot pasta to sauce and toss lightly until evenly mixed. Place in a warm serving bowl and sprinkle with green onions.

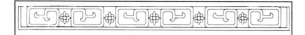

Fettuccine with Shrimp and Squid

Makes 4 to 6 servings

Lobster Sauce
3 cups water
1/4 cup dry white wine
1/4 cup distilled white vinegar
1 small stalk celery, chopped
1/2 small carrot, chopped
1/2 small onion, chopped
1/2 teaspoon salt
1/4 teaspoon whole black peppers
1/2 bay leaf
1/8 teaspoon dried thyme leaves
1/4 cup lobster base
3 tablespoons cornstarch
4 tablespoons water

8 ounces fettuccine
2 tablespoons vegetable oil
1/2 pound medium raw shrimp, shelled
    and deveined
2 tablespoons minced garlic
2 tablespoons minced shallots
1 pound small squid, cleaned, with tentacles
    separated and body cut in 1/4-inch rings
4 green onions (white part only), cut into
    1-inch pieces
1/4 cup dry white wine
1 medium tomato, peeled and diced

*D*uring food preparation, we save lobster shells to use in this sauce and you can do that too. As a shortcut, you can also buy lobster base, a dry product similar to chicken stock base, in grocery stores and fish markets.

In a 2 to 3-quart pan combine the 3 cups water, wine, vinegar, celery, carrot, onion, salt, black peppers, bay leaf, and thyme. Bring to a boil; cover, reduce heat, and simmer for 30 minutes. Strain stock; discard solids. Return stock to pan and place over medium heat. Dissolve lobster base in stock. In a bowl mix cornstarch and the 4 tablespoons water. Add to stock and cook, stirring, until sauce thickens enough to coat a spoon.

Cook pasta in a large kettle of boiling salted water according to package directions until barely tender to bite. Drain.

While pasta is cooking, heat oil in a wide frying pan over medium heat. Add shrimp, garlic, and shallots; cook, stirring for 2 minutes. Add squid and cook for 1 minute. Add green onions, wine, lobster sauce, and tomato. Heat through.

Place pasta in a warm serving bowl, pour sauce over pasta, and toss.

Ziti with Fresh Tomato and Olives

Makes 4 servings

8 ounces ziti or mostaccioli (penne) pasta
2 tablespoons olive oil
1 small onion, chopped
1 teaspoon minced garlic
1 teaspoon minced shallot
1 cup sliced mushrooms
1 teaspoon dried oregano leaves
1 can (2 1/4 ounces) sliced ripe olives
Salt and freshly ground pepper
1 large tomato, peeled and diced
1 cup grated Parmesan cheese

If you're looking for a well-flavored meatless pasta, try this one dressed with mushrooms, olives, and tomato. Boil the water to cook the pasta first: the sauce can be prepared in minutes.

Cook pasta in a large kettle of boiling salted water according to package directions until barely tender to bite. Drain.

While pasta is cooking, heat oil in a wide frying pan over medium heat. Add onion, garlic, and shallot. Cook, stirring occasionally, until onion is soft, about 4 minutes. Add mushrooms and oregano. Cook for 2 minutes. Add olives and salt and pepper to taste. Add tomto and hot pasta to sauce, toss gently, and cook for 1 minute. Place pasta in a warm serving bowl and sprinkle with Parmesan cheese.

Note: Ziti is tubular macaroni, sometimes sold long, then broken into pieces to cook. You can use any other medium-shaped pasta for this recipe.

Red Pepper Fettuccine and Corn in Achiote Tomato Sauce

Makes 6 servings

1 pound red pepper fettuccine or regular
    fettuccine
2 tablespoons olive oil
3 cups fresh corn (about 6 large ears corn,
    husked and scraped)
1 teaspoon minced garlic
2 cups diced peeled tomatoes (3 medium
    tomatoes)
Achiote Tomato Sauce (facing page)
1 cup julienned strips jicama
1/4 cup sliced ripe olives
1/4 cup chopped green onions
1 lime, halved
Salt and pepper

The vibrant flavors and colors of Southwest cuisine inspired the bold sauce for this pasta. At Fat City we serve it with fettuccine flavored with roasted red bell peppers, but it is equally good served over regular fettuccine. It's best to cook dried pasta for this recipe. Fresh pasta is too delicate for the sauce.

Cook pasta in a large kettle of boiling salted water according to package directions until barely tender to bite. Drain.

While pasta is cooking, heat oil in a wide frying pan over medium heat. Add corn and cook until heated through, about 2 minutes. Add garlic and cook for 1 minute. Add tomatoes and achiote sauce. When sauce is hot, add jicama, olives, and green onions. Cook until sauce simmers. Squeeze juice from lime halves into sauce and add salt and pepper to taste.

Place pasta on a warm serving platter. Pour sauce over pasta and serve.

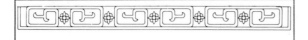

Achiote Tomato Sauce

Makes 3 cups sauce

1/4 cup annatto seeds
3 3/4 cups tomato juice
2 tablespoons lemon juice
2 tablespoons olive oil
1 1/2 teaspoons minced garlic
1 1/2 teaspoons ground cumin
1 1/2 teapoons dried oregano leaves
1 1/2 teaspoons sugar

*T*iny achiote seeds, harvested from the tropical annatto tree, are basic to Southwest and Philippine cooking. Like paprika, achiote adds a subtle earthy flavor and brick red color which complements fish, poultry, and vegetables. Look for annatto seeds in the Mexican food section of supermarkets.

Place annatto seeds in a bowl with boiling water to cover; cover and let stand 2 hours to soften seeds. Drain. In a blender combine 3/4 cup of the tomato juice, lemon juice, olive oil, annatto seeds, garlic, cumin, and oregano. Smoothly puree, 4 to 5 minutes. Sauce will thicken slightly as the annatto seeds absorb the liquid. Transfer to a 2-quart pan.

Add the remaining 3 cups tomato juice and sugar. Bring to a boil; reduce heat and simmer, stirring frequently to prevent scorching, until sauce has been reduced to 3 cups, 10 to 20 minutes.

Note: This is an excellent sauce to serve over grilled fish.

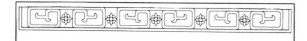

Vegetable Lasagne

Makes 8 servings

Tomato Sauce
1/4 cup olive oil
1 medium onion, chopped
1 tablespoon chopped garlic
5 large tomatoes, peeled and chopped
2 tablespoons chopped fresh basil or 2 teaspoons
    dried basil
1 tablespoon chopped fresh oregano or
    1 teaspoon dried oregano
1/4 cup dry red wine
1 tablespoon tomato paste
Salt

White Sauce
3 tablespoons butter
1/4 cup all-purpose flour
1 cup milk
1 cup heavy cream
Salt and white pepper

1 tablespoon olive oil
3 large onions, chopped
3 green bell peppers, seeded and thinly
    sliced into rings
1 1/2 pounds mushrooms, sliced
2 pounds zucchini, sliced crosswise
1 teaspoon salt
1/2 teaspoon pepper
16 to 20 lasagne noodles
1 cup grated Parmesan cheese

Many customers look for meatless options on our menus. One of Fat City's answers to a satisfying vegetarian entree is this flavorful lasagne.

For the tomato sauce, heat oil in a 2 to 3-quart pan over medium heat. Add onion and garlic and cook until onion is soft, 4 to 5 minutes. Add tomatoes, basil, and oregano. Cover and simmer, stirring occasionally, for 30 minutes. Stir in wine and tomato paste. Cover and simmer 30 more minutes, stirring occasionally, until sauce has thickened. Add salt to taste; set aside.

For the white sauce, melt butter in another 2-quart pan over medium heat. Add flour and cook, stirring, until roux is bubbly but not browned. Using a whisk, blend in milk and cream until smooth. Stirring, cook until sauce is smooth, boiling, and lightly thickened. Correct seasoning with salt and pepper; set aside.

Heat oil in a 5-quart kettle over medium-high heat. Add onions and cook until limp, 8 to 10 minutes. Add bell peppers, mushrooms, and zucchini. Cook, stirring occasionally, until vegetables are tender but not mushy, about 10 minutes. Add salt and pepper. Drain excess pan juices. Mixture should be moist but not runny.

Cook lasagne noodles in a large kettle of boiling salted water according to package directions until barely tender to bite. Drain, rinse with cold water, and drain again. Grease a 9 by 13-inch baking dish. Spread a thin layer of tomato sauce over the bottom. Arrange 1/3 of the noodles over the sauce. Spread 1/3 of vegetable mixture over noodles; top with 1/3 of the white sauce, then cover with 1/3 of tomato sauce. Repeat this layering two more times, ending with tomato sauce. Sprinkle Parmesan cheese over the top.

Bake, covered, in a 350° F oven for 30 minutes. Uncover and continue to bake until hot and bubbly, 10 to 15 minutes. Cut into squares to serve.

Poultry

Chicken in a "Fat" Pot

Chicken Pignolia

Chicken in Black Bean Sauce

Chicken Breasts with Curry Sauce

Olallieberry Chicken

Chicken Dijon

Chicken with Port Wine Sauce

Peppered Chicken

Wild Rice-Stuffed Chicken Breasts

Steamed Garlic Chicken

Smoked Chicken with Fragrant Fruits

Garlic Game Hens

Roast Honey-glazed Duck

Coconut-Curried Turkey Lasagne

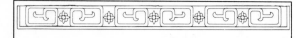

Chicken in a "Fat" Pot

Makes 2 or 3 servings

Marinade
1 1/2 teaspoons soy sauce
1 1/2 teaspoons brandy
1 1/2 teaspoons minced fresh ginger
1/2 teaspoon sugar
1/2 teaspoon sesame oil

3/4 pound boneless, skinless chicken breasts,
  cut into 3/4-inch cubes

Sauce
1/2 cup chicken broth
2 tablespoons oyster sauce
2 tablespoons soy sauce
1/8 teaspoon white pepper
1/8 teaspoon sesame oil

2 1/2 tablespoons vegetable oil
2 tablespoons dry sherry
1/2 cup quartered fresh mushrooms
1 cup cut vegetables such as asparagus, bell
  pepper, zucchini, and carrot, cut into uniform bite-size pieces (if using carrot, blanch
  in boiling water for 2 minutes)
1 1/2 teaspoons cornstarch dissolved in
  1 tablespoon water
Hot steamed rice

*S*tir-fries never go out of style so when China Camp reopened as California Fats, we kept this popular dish on the menu and updated the presentation only: crisp-tender vegetables and juicy nuggets of chicken, accented with oyster sauce, are served in an individual casserole or "fat" pot over rice. It's simple, wholesome, and utterly delicious.

Combine marinade ingredients in a medium bowl. Add chicken and stir to coat; cover and refrigerate for 2 hours. Combine sauce ingredients in a small bowl; set aside.

Place a wok or wide frying pan over high heat until hot. Add 2 tablespoons of the oil, swirling to coat the sides. Add the chicken and stir-fry until opaque, about 2 minutes. Add sherry and toss with chicken; remove chicken from pan.

Add the remaining 1/2 tablespoon oil to pan. Add vegetables and stir-fry for 1 minute. Stir in sauce and bring to a boil. Return chicken to pan. Add cornstarch solution and cook, stirring, until sauce boils and thickens slightly. Serve over rice.

Note: When you marinate food, use a bowl or pan with a nonreactive finish such as stainless steel or glass. Aluminum tend to react with acidic foods causing a slight metallic flavor.

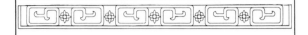

Chicken Pignolia

Makes 4 servings

Sweet and Sour Sauce
1 cup sugar
1 cup each white wine vinegar and water
3/4 cup catsup
5 tablespoons A-1 sauce
1/4 cup Worcestershire sauce
2 tablespoons soy sauce
1 tablespoon lemon juice
1/2 teaspoon ginger juice (squeeze from grated
    fresh ginger)
1/8 teaspoon salt

Marinade
1 egg white
1/2 cup water
2 teaspoons cornstarch
2 teaspoons dry white wine
2 teapoons minced fresh ginger
1/2 teaspoon each salt and sugar
Dash each of white pepper and sesame oil
2 tablespoons vegetable oil

1 pound boneless, skinless chicken thighs, cut
    into 3/4 inch cubes
2 tablespoons vegetable oil
1/2 cup pinenuts
1/2 cup diced onion
1 teapoon minced garlic
1 each green and red bell pepper, seeded and
    diced
1/4 cup diced zucchini
Hot steamed rice

The flavors of this stir-fry are fresh and simple, and the sauce has a lighter, more fruity flavor than the usual sweet and sour sauce. Don't save the sauce just for chicken. It's good on crispy-fried fish fillets too.

Prepare the sauce: Combine all ingredients in a 2-quart pan. Bring to a boil over medium heat; stir frequently until sugar is dissolved. Reduce heat to low and simmer, uncovered, until sauce is reduced to 2 cups, 10 to 15 minutes; set 1 cup of sauce aside. Reserve remaining sauce to use another time.

Combine all marinade ingredients except oil in a bowl and whisk lightly with a fork; add oil. Add chicken and stir to coat; cover and refrigerate for 1 hour.

Heat oil in a wok or wide frying pan over low heat. Add pine nuts and cook, stirring frequently, until golden brown, about 2 minutes. Remove with a slotted spoon and drain on a paper towel.

Increase heat to high. When oil is almost smoking, add chicken, onion, and garlic. Stir-fry for 1 minute. Add bell peppers and zucchini. Stir-fry for 2 minutes or until chicken is opaque and vegtables are crisp-tender. Stir in sweet and sour sauce and cook until sauce is heated through. Serve over rice and sprinkle with pine nuts.

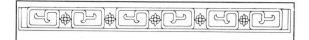

Chicken in Black Bean Sauce

Makes 3 or 4 servings

Sauce
1/4 cup chicken broth
1 tablespoon oyster sauce
1 tablespoon soy sauce
1/2 teaspoon sesame oil

3/4 pound boneless, skinless chicken breasts,
    thinly sliced
2 tablespoons cornstarch
2 tablespoons vegetable oil
1 tablespoon minced garlic
1 tablespoon minced shallot
3 medium zucchini, cut in matchstick pieces
1 red or green bell pepper, seeded and
    thinly sliced
4 asparagus spears, tough ends discarded, cut in
    1 1/2-inch diagonal slices
2 tablespoons preserved black beans, rinsed,
    drained, and chopped

Chockful of vegetables, this traditional chicken stir-fry served with noodles or rice makes an easy one-dish meal. If you cook Chinese egg noodles, heat a pot of water while you cut the vegetables. Drop the noodles in the boiling water as you heat your wok. The noodles and chicken should cook in about the same length of time.

Combine sauce ingredients in a small bowl; set aside. Dredge chicken in cornstarch; shake off excess.

Place a wok or wide frying pan over high heat until hot. Add oil, swirling to coat the sides. Add chicken, garlic, and shallot. Stir-fry for 1 minute. Add zucchini, bell pepper, asparagus, and black beans. Stir-fry for 1 minute. Add sauce. Stir-fry for 2 minutes or until vegetables are crisp-tender and chicken is opaque.

Note: If your equipment does not generate high heat, cook the components of a stir-fry in sequence. First cook poultry, meat, or seafood until three-fourths done and remove from the wok. Next stir-fry vegetables until crisp-tender. Return the meat to the wok and add sauce. The meat will complete cooking as the sauce heats. If a recipe calls for cornstarch-water thickener, give the cornstarch-water mixture a stir to recombine, add to the pan at the final stage of cooking, and cook, stirring, until sauce bubbles and thickens slightly.

Chicken Breasts with Curry Sauce

Makes 4 servings

Curry Sauce
1 cup unsweetened coconut milk
1/2 cup chicken broth
2 tablespoons curry powder
1 tablespoon butter
Salt and white pepper

4 teaspoons minced garlic
4 teaspoons minced shallot
1 teaspoon salt
1/2 teaspoon pepper
4 tablespoons curry power
1 tablespoon ground cumin
4 large chicken breast halves, boned, with
    skin on
2 tablespoons olive oil

$\mathcal{M}$emories of heavenly curries tasted in Southeast Asia inspired this version of chicken. For consistency, we use a good quality curry powder rather than grind a half dozen spices with a mortar and pestle. This control ensures a deep-flavored, silken-textured sauce time after time after time. For a more elaborate presentation, you could offer side dishes of chutney, roasted almonds, raisins, and coconut.

Prepare the sauce: Combine coconut milk and chicken broth in a small pan. Cook over medium heat until sauce has reduced enough to coat a spoon, about 10 minutes. Whisk in curry powder and cook for 1 minute. Stir in butter. Remove sauce from the heat and correct seasoning with salt and pepper.

Combine garlic, shallot, salt, and pepper in a small bowl. In a wide shallow bowl, mix curry powder and cumin. Rub garlic mixture over each piece of chicken; dredge chicken in curry mixture.

Heat oil in a wide frying pan over medium heat. Place chicken in pan, skin side down, and cook for 5 minutes. Turn chicken over and cook until meat in thickest part is no longer pink when cut, about 5 more minutes.

To serve, reheat curry sauce. Place a spoonful of sauce on each plate. Place chicken on top of the sauce.

Note: Like heavy cream which rises to the top of unhomogenized milk, a creamy thick layer called coconut cream rises to the top of coconut milk. Shake canned coconut milk well before opening to reblend the contents. Once opened, canned coconut milk lasts 2 to 3 days under refrigeration. You can freeze it for longer storage.

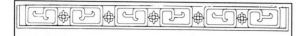

Olallieberry Chicken

Makes 4 servings

Olallieberry Sauce
1 teaspoon vegetable oil
1/2 small onion, chopped
2 cups chicken broth
2 cups olallieberries
1 tablespoon cornstarch dissolved in
    1 tablespoon wildberry brandy and
    1 tablespoon water
1 1/2 teaspoons brown sugar
1 1/2 teaspoons lemon juice
1/4 teaspoon salt
1/8 teaspoon white pepper

4 large chicken breast halves, boned and skinned
2 tablespoons raspberry vinegar
1 teaspoon salt
1/2 teaspoon pepper
3 tablespoons olive oil

*T*his recipe has gone through transition. Originally made with raspberries, we adapted it to ollalieberries when we found a source for the luscious shiny black berries. Wildberry brandy intensifies the fruity flavor.

Prepare the sauce: Heat oil in a 2-quart pan over medium heat. Add onion and cook until soft. Add chicken broth and berries. Bring to a boil; reduce heat and simmer, uncovered, for 15 minutes. In a blender, smoothly puree berry mixture. Push the puree through a sieve and discard seeds. Return puree to pan. Add cornstarch solution and cook, stirring, until sauce boils and thickens slightly. Add brown sugar, lemon juice, salt, and pepper. Over low heat, simmer sauce until it is the consistency of tomato sauce. Set aside.

With a mallet, lightly pound chicken breasts to 1/2 inch thickness. Place in a wide shallow bowl; pour vinegar over breasts. Cover and refrigerate overnight; turn breasts once or twice. Just before cooking, drain breasts and pat dry with paper towels. Sprinkle with salt and pepper.

Heat oil in a wide frying pan over medium heat. Place breasts in pan and cook, turning once, until chicken is lightly browned and no long pink when cut, 8 to 10 minutes total.

To serve, reheat olallieberry sauce. Place a spoonful of sauce on each plate. Place chicken on top of the sauce.

Note: Developed at Oregon State University and now grown extensively in California, olallieberries are a cross between a black loganberry and young berry. The season runs May through July. To freeze for longer use, place unwashed berries in a single layer on a shallow pan; freeze solid. Transfer to plastic bags and return to the freezer. Rinse berries while still frozen before using.

Chicken Dijon

Makes 4 servings

4 large chicken breast halves, boned and skinned
Salt and pepper
All-purpose flour
1/2 cup heavy cream
2 tablespoons Dijon mustard
4 tablespoons butter
1 tablespoon brandy
1 tablespoon minced shallot
1 tablespoon minced garlic
1/2 cup sliced mushrooms
2 teaspoons finely chopped parsley

Chicken breasts sauteed to moist perfection are topped with a creamy mustard sauce quickly made in the same pan. Using a wok-cooking technique, the chicken is splashed with brandy before the sauce is made. This allows the alcohol to evaporate and the brandy flavor to penetrate the meat.

Sprinkle breasts with salt and pepper; dredge in flour, shaking off excess. In a small bowl, whisk together cream and mustard; set aside.

Melt butter in a wide frying pan over medium heat. When butter sizzles, add chicken and cook, turning once, until chicken is golden and no longer pink when cut, 8 to 10 minutes total. Splash chicken with brandy. Transfer to a platter and keep warm.

Add shallot and garlic to pan drippings. Cook for 1 minute. Add mushrooms and parsley. Cook until mushrooms have released their liquid and pan juices have evaporated. Stir in mustard cream mixture. Simmer until sauce thickens slightly. Pour sauce over chicken and serve.

Chicken with Port Wine Sauce

Makes 4 servings

1/2 cup small whole mushrooms
2 cups chicken broth
1 cup port wine
2 teaspoons cracked black pepper
1 1/2 teaspoons chopped fresh thyme or
    1/2 teapoon dried thyme
1 bay leaf
4 large chicken breast halves, boned and skinned
1/2 cup green or red seedless grapes
1 1/2 teaspoons cornstarch dissolved in
    1 tablespoon water
Salt and pepper

*I*ntensely fruity best describes chicken breasts first poached in port wine stock, then topped with a port wine reduction and grapes.

Rinse mushrooms and remove stems. Set caps aside and place stems in a 2-quart pan. To mushroom stems add chicken broth, wine, pepper, thyme, and bay leaf. Bring to a boil; reduce heat and simmer, uncovered, until sauce is reduced to 2 cups.

Place breasts in pan with sauce and reheat to simmering. Cover and simmer until meat is no long pink when cut in the thickest part, 15 to 20 minutes. Lift out breasts with a slotted spoon and place on a serving platter; keep warm.

Bring sauce to a boil; reduce heat and simmer, uncovered, until reduced to 1 cup. Strain sauce and return to pan. Add mushroom caps and grapes. Cook for 1 minute. Add cornstarch solution and cook, stirring, until sauce boils and thickens slightly. Correct seasoning with salt and pepepr. Pour sauce over chicken and serve.

Peppered Chicken

Makes 4 servings

4 large chicken breast halves, boned and skinned
1 teaspoon sichuan peppercorns, lightly crushed
1 teaspoon cracked black pepper
Salt
1/2 cup heavy cream
1 teaspoon Dijon mustard
1 tablespoon olive oil
1 tablespoon brandy
1/2 cup chicken broth
1 teaspoon green peppercorns and juice

Quick, easy, and elegant, this makes a fine company entree. You might serve it with Herbed Potatoes (page 133), and for color, fresh asparagus or tiny green beans.

With a mallet, lightly pound chicken breasts to 1/2 inch thickness. Mix sichuan peppercorns and black pepper in a small bowl. Sprinkle chicken lightly with salt; press pepper mixture on both sides of breasts. In a small bowl, whisk together cream and mustard; set aside.

Heat oil in a wide frying pan over medium heat. Add chicken and cook, turning once, until chicken is lightly browned and no longer pink when cut, 8 to 10 minutes total. Splash chicken with brandy; transfer to a platter and keep warm.

Deglaze pan with chicken broth, stirring to scrape up browned bits. When broth simmers, add mustard cream and cook until sauce bubbles and thickens slightly. Stir in green peppercorns. Pour sauce over chicken and serve.

Note: Sichuan peppercorns are not true peppercorns, but dried berries of an unrelated plant. They have a pronounced aroma and mildly hot taste, spicier than black peppercorns, but not fiery hot like chiles.

Cracked black pepper is a coarsely ground pepper widely available in small bottles in supermarket spice selections. It has a more pungent flavor than regular ground pepper.

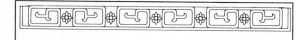

Wild Rice-Stuffed Chicken Breasts

Makes 4 servings

1/2 cup wild rice
5 tablespoons butter
1/2 cup chopped onion
3 cups chicken broth
1/2 cup grated Parmesan cheese
4 large chicken breast halves, boned and skinned
Salt and pepper
1 cup sliced mushrooms
3/4 cup heavy cream
1 teaspoon chopped fresh chervil or
    1/2 teaspoon dried chervil
1 tablespoon lemon juice
1 tablespoon cold butter

It's not uncommon for Chinese cooks to use several cooking techniques to achieve a specific result, and I have done this here. Boned chicken breasts are rolled around a stuffing, wrapped in foil, and steamed briefly to set the shape. The meat is exceptionally moist but pale. To give a browned finish more suitable to Western tastes, the chicken in sauteed in butter and bathed in a creamy herb sauce.

In a bowl cover wild rice with water and let soak for 2 hours; drain. Melt 2 tablespoons of the butter in a 2-quart pan. Add onion and cook until onion is soft, 3 to 4 minutes. Add 2 cups of the chicken broth and wild rice. Cover and bring to a boil; reduce heat and simmer for 20 or until wild rice is tender and all liquid has been absorbed. Remove from heat and stir in cheese; set aside.

Butterfly each breast by cutting in half horizontally almost all the way through, leaving one long edge attached. Spread each breast open like a book and place between 2 sheets of wax paper. With a mallet gently pound breasts to 1/4 inch thickness.

Season breasts with salt and pepper. To make each roll, place 1/4 of rice mixture in center of each breast. Fold lower edge of breast over filling, then fold in sides and roll up to enclose filling. Individually wrap chicken rolls tightly in a square of plastic wrap; twist ends to seal. Place rolls in a glass pie dish.

Place a steaming rack in a wok, add water to just below level of rack, and bring to a boil. Place the dish on the rack, cover, and steam for 8 minutes. Remove the dish from the wok and let cool. Unwrap chicken rolls and discard plastic wrap.

Melt the remaining 3 tablespoons butter in a wide frying pan over medium heat. When butter sizzles, add chicken rolls and cook, turning to brown lightly on all sides, 5 to 7 minutes. Move chicken to one side of pan, add mushrooms, and cook for 1 minute. Add the remaining 1 cup chicken broth and simmer 1 minute. Add cream and chervil and simmer until sauce has thickened enough to coat a spoon.

With a slotted spatula, transfer chicken rolls to a warm serving platter. Stir lemon juice into sauce. Remove pan from heat and stir in butter. When butter melts, pour sauce over chicken and serve.

Steamed Garlic Chicken

Makes 4 servings

Marinade
2 tablespoons brandy
4 teaspoons soy sauce
1 teaspoon sugar
1 teaspoon ginger juice, squeezed from grated
    fresh ginger
1/2 teaspoon white pepper

4 large chicken breast halves, boned, with
    skin on
1/2 cup Virginia ham or other sugar-cured
    baked ham cut in thin strips
4 green onions, white part only, cut in thin strips
1 tablespoon slivered fresh ginger
2 tablespoons water
1 tablespoon cornstarch
2 to 4 drops sesame oil

Sauce
2 teaspoons vegetable oil
2 tablespoons minced garlic
1/4 cup finely chopped green onion
1 teaspoon minced fresh rosemary or 1/4
    teaspoon dried rosemary
1/2 teaspoon white pepper
1 cup chicken broth
1 tablespoon cornstarch dissolved in
    2 tablespoons water

Minced chives

*T*he Chinese relish steamed chicken. We love its velvety texture and ivory colored skin. At home, we chop the whole bird with a cleaver and serve it bones and all. For California Fats I wanted a dish that would duplicate the succulent meat but be easier to serve and eat. Boneless breasts rolled up with ham and green onions are the result. Rosemary gives a non-Asian sparkle to the light clear sauce.

Combine marinade ingredients in a wide shallow bowl. With a mallet, lightly pound breasts to 1/2 inch thickness. Place breasts in marinade and turn to coat. Cover and refrigerate 2 hours, turning once.

Place chicken, skin side down, on work surface. Across each breast place 1/4 of the ham, green onions, and ginger. In a bowl combine water, cornstarch, and sesame oil. Roll each breast into a tight cylinder, making sure part of the filling is exposed at the ends. Brush cornstarch mixture over rolled chicken. Place chicken, seam side down, in a glass pie dish.

Place a steaming rack in a wok, add water to just below level of rack, and bring to a boil. Place the dish on the rack, cover, and steam until chicken is no longer pink when cut, 10 to 12 minutes. (Cut a tiny slit to test.) Remove the dish from the wok; carefully pour the cooking juices into a cup and reserve.

To make the sauce, heat oil in a small frying pan over medium heat. Add garlic and cook 30 seconds or until fragrant. Add green onion, rosemary, and pepper. Cook for 30 seconds. Add chicken broth and reserved cooking juices. Bring sauce to a simmer and cook until it has reduced to about 1 cup. Add cornstarch solution and cook, stirring, until sauce boils and thickens slightly.

To serve, arrange chicken rolls on a platter. Strain sauce over chicken and garnish with chives.

Smoked Chicken with Fragrant Fruits

Makes 8 servings

*2 pounds smoked breast of chicken, boned
    and diced*
*1/2 cup diced melon (cantaloupe, honeydew,
    or a mixture)*
1/4 cup diced fresh pineapple
1/4 cup red or green seedless grapes, halved
1/4 cup diced peeled green apple
1/4 cup sweet pickled red ginger strips
1/2 cup chicken broth
1/2 teaspoon each oyster sauce and soy sauce
1/4 teaspoon sesame oil
Dash of white pepper
8 purchased patty shells (puff pastry shells)
Fresh mint sprigs

This beautiful entree is perfect to star at a brunch or weekend luncheon. Smoke the chicken in a covered barbecue if you wish, or buy a hickory-smoked chicken at a supermarket deli.

Heat a wide frying pan with a nonstick finish over medium heat. Add chicken, melon, pineapple, grapes, apple, and ginger. Stir gently and cook until mixture is hot. Transfer to a large bowl.

Add chicken broth to pan. When it comes to a boil, stir in oyster sauce, soy sauce, sesame oil, and pepper. Reduce heat to low; simmer sauce for 1 minute. Return chicken-fruit mixture to pan. Stir gently to evenly mix. To serve, divide chicken and fruit into patty shells. Garnish each with a sprig of mint.

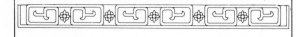

Garlic Game Hens

Makes 4 servings

4 Rock Cornish game hens (1 to
*   1 1/2 pounds each)*
Salt and pepper
1 lemon, cut in quarters
30 cloves garlic, crushed with blade of a knife
*   and peeled*
1 bunch cilantro (Chinese parsley),
*   coarsely chopped*
1 cup coarsely chopped mixed fresh herbs:
*   marjoram, oregano, and thyme*
1/4 cup olive oil
1/4 cup white wine vinegar
1/4 cup soy sauce
1/4 cup light corn syrup

Roasted whole, small-scale game hens make elegant individual servings . They are a good size too for eat-with-your-fingers picnicking. Because these young birds have a mild flavor, I stuff them with a generous amount of garlic and herbs.

Remove game hens necks and giblets; reserve for other uses. Rinse hens inside and out; pat dry. Rub salt and pepper inside of each hen. Squeeze the juice of 1 lemon quarter in each body cavity; place lemon quarters in hens. In a bowl, toss garlic with cilantro and herbs. Stuff one-fourth of herb mixture in each hen. Close cavities with small metal skewers.

Combine olive oil, wine vinegar, soy sauce, and corn syrup in a bowl. Generously brush over hens. Place hens, breast up, on a rack in a foil-lined shallow roasting pan. Basting frequently with oil mixture, roast in a 375° F oven for 1 to 1 1/2 hours, depending on size of hens, or until meat near thighbone is no long pink when slashed. Remove hens from oven, cover loosely with foil, and let stand for 10 minutes so juices will settle back into the meat. Remove skewers and stuffing before serving.

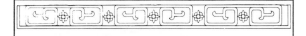

Roast Honey-glazed Duck

Makes 4 servings

Marinade
1/4 cup oyster sauce
1/4 cup hoisin sauce
1/4 cup brandy
1/4 cup anisette liqueur
1 tablespoon sugar
1 teaspoon five-spice powder
1/4 teaspoon each salt and pepper
1 whole star anise

1 duck (muscovy or domestic), 4 to 5 pounds, dressed

Honey Glaze
3/4 cup red wine vinegar
3/4 cup distilled white vinegar
3/4 cup water
1/2 cup honey

Raspberry-duck Sauce
2 cups water
1 cup sugar
1/2 cup raspberry vinegar
1 cup fresh raspberries
1/4 cup raspberry liqueur
1 tablespoon butter

In the Chinese cuisine, crispy-skinned roast duck is a time-honored favorite.

Combine marinade ingredients in a bowl and mix well. If head is missing from duck, sew neck opening with string so marinade will not leak out. Pour marinade in duck cavity. Seal closed with string or skewer.

In a pan over medium heat, combine honey glaze ingredients. Stir while heating until honey is dissolved.

Heat a wok or large pan with enough water to cover the duck. When water comes to a boil, turn off heat. Blanch duck on both sides in water, about 1 minute. Drain duck and place on a rack in a roasting pan. Brush on all sides with honey glaze. Refrigerate uncovered and allow glaze to dry for 48 hours.

Prepare raspberry-duck sauce: In a 2-quart pan, bring water, sugar, and vinegar to a boil; stir occasionally until sugar dissolves. Reduce heat and simmer, uncovered, until mixture is like heavy syrup. Add raspberries and liqueur; cook for 1 minute. In a blender, smoothly puree berry mixture. Push puree through a sieve and discard seeds. Return puree to pan and stir in butter. Set sauce aside.

Roast duck in a preheated 375° F oven for 20 minutes per pound. To test doneness, insert a skewer into thigh area. The juices should run clear. The skin should be golden brown and crispy. Cut duck into serving size pieces and serve with raspberry-duck sauce.

Wine recommendation: A medium to full bodied merlot marries with the sweet richness of the duck.

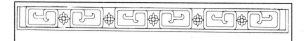

Coconut-Curried Turkey Lasagne

Makes 8 servings

Coconut-Curry Sauce
2 cups chicken broth
1 can (14 ounces) unsweetened coconut milk
1 tablespoon curry powder
1 teaspoon salt
1 teaspoon dry mustard
1/2 teaspoon sugar
1/8 teaspoon crushed dried red chiles

12 to 16 lasagne noodles
2 tablespoons vegetable oil
1/4 cup chopped shallots
1 tablespoon minced garlic
1 cup diced onion
1 cup diced celery
*1 each green and red bell pepper, seeded
    and diced*
*1 tablespoon chopped fresh marjoram or
    1 teaspoon dried marjoram*
3 cups diced cooked turkey
1/2 teaspoon salt
1/4 teaspoon pepper
3/4 pound peppered jack cheese, shredded

My version of lasagne has a mixed geographical heritage: layered pasta from Italy, silky coconut-curry sauce from Southeast Asia, and peppered jack cheese from California. It adds up to a wonderful make-ahead dish for casual entertaining.

Prepare the sauce: Combine chicken broth and coconut milk in a 2-quart pan and cook, uncovered, over medium heat for 10 minutes. Add remaining sauce ingredients. Simmer for 10 minutes or until sauce is reduced to 2 cups.

Cook lasagne noodles in a large kettle of boiling salted water according to package directions until barely tender to bite. Drain, rinse with cold water, and drain again.

Heat oil in a wide frying pan over medium heat. Add shallots and garlic and cook for 30 seconds. Add onion, celery, bell peppers, and marjoram. Cook until onion is soft, 8 to 10 minutes. Add turkey, salt, and pepper; mix well.

Grease a 9 by 13-inch baking dish. Spread a thin layer of sauce over the bottom. Arrange 1/3 of the noodles over the sauce. Spread 1/3 of turkey mixture over noodles; top with 1/3 of the sauce, then sprinkle with 1/3 of the cheese. Repeat this layering two more times ending with cheese. Bake, covered, in a 350° F oven for 30 minutes. Uncover and continue to bake until hot and bubbly, 10 to 15 minutes. Cut into squares to serve.

Note: Coconut milk is a creamy liquid made by steeping grated coconut meat in hot water, then straining it through cheesecloth. For convenience we use canned unsweetened coconut milk. Brands from Thailand work well because they have a consistent ratio of coconut milk to coconut cream.

Seafood

Steamed Salmon in Ti Leaves

Stuffed Coho Salmon with Ginger Sauce

Pacific Snapper with Herb Butter-Caper Sauce

Grilled Ahi Tuna with Papaya Relish

Trout with Beer Brown Butter

Baked Sea Bass with Lemon-Butter Sauce

Asparagus Prawns with Black Bean Sauce

Lobster Soong

Butterflied SesameShrimp

Shrimp Nori

Crab Cakes with Chile-Cream Sauce

Steamed Salmon in Ti Leaves

Makes 4 servings

2 tablespoons preserved black beans, rinsed,
    drained, and chopped
2 tablespoons minced garlic
4 ti leaves
About 1 1/2 pounds salmon fillet, skinned and
    cut into 4 portions
4 green onions and tops, thinly sliced
4 thin slices fresh ginger, slivered

Chile-Soy Sauce
1/4 cup vegetable oil
2 teaspoons minced, seeded small hot chile such
    as fresh jalapeño
2 teaspoons sesame oil
1/4 cup soy sauce

*T*he cooking technique and seasoning for this dish is traditional Chinese, the presentation Western. When I decided to introduce steamed fish at California Fats, I knew that our customers preferred fish without bones, but a steamed salmon fillet, while delicious to eat, looks rather plain and uninteresting. Then I remembered laulaus, the Hawaiian specialty which is wrapped in ti leaves and steamed in a pit. For our stove-top steaming, ti leaves now provide the packaging that gives extra sizzle to a spectacular tasting dish.

With a chef's knife, finely chop black beans and garlic together to make a rough paste. To make each packet, place a ti leaf on work surface vein side up. Place a piece of salmon on leaf; spread with 1 tablespoon black bean paste. Sprinkle with one-fourth of the green onions and one-fourth of the ginger. Wrap both ends of ti leaf around salmon to completely enclose. Ends of packet will be open.

Prepare the sauce: Warm vegetable oil in a small pan over low heat. Remove from heat and add minced chile and sesame oil. Stir in soy sauce (the oil will sizzle). Remove pan from heat.

Place a bamboo steaming basket or steaming rack in a wok, add water to just below level of basket, and bring to a boil. Place packets in basket, cover, and steam until the center of fish is opaque, 7 to 10 minutes. To test, cut a tiny slit through a ti leaf into the fish. Transfer the fish to a platter or 4 dinner plates. Open ti leaves and tuck edges under the fish. Serve fish with warm chile-soy sauce for dipping.

Note: Ti leaves are widely available from florists. If you cannot find ti leaves, wrap each portion of salmon in a 12-inch square of aluminum foil.

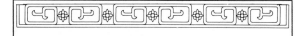

Stuffed Coho Salmon with Ginger Sauce

Makes 4 servings

2 dried Chinese black mushrooms
1/4 pound small raw shrimp, shelled
    and deveined
1/4 pound ground lean pork
2 tablespoons sliced bamboo shoots
2 tablespoons sliced green onion
1 teaspoon soy sauce
1/8 teaspoon each salt and white pepper
4 farm-raised coho (7 to 8 ounces each), boned
All-purpose flour
3 tablespoons vegetable oil

Ginger Sauce
2 cups chicken broth
1 teaspoon minced ginger
1 tablespoon soy sauce
1/2 teaspoon each salt and sugar
1 tablespoon brandy
1 tablespoon cornstarch dissolved in
    2 tablespoons water
Salt and white pepper

In Western cooking, a stuffing for fish is typically based on bread, onion, and celery. Chinese cooks prefer to stuff fish with a richer, more flavorful mixture such as this one pairing shrimp and pork. The clear ginger sauce provides a smooth contrast to the crispy-skin fish. If you wish to give this a dressier presentation, garnish the serving platter with a ring of shredded green onion.

Preheat oven to 375° F. Soak mushrooms in warm water to cover for 30 minutes; drain. Cut off stems, roughly slice caps, and place in a food processor. To the mushrooms add shrimp, pork, bamboo shoots, green onion, soy sauce, salt, and white pepper. Process to make a rough paste.

Rinse fish under running water; pat dry with paper towels. Spread one-fourth of shrimp mixture in a thin layer inside of each fish. Dredge fish with flour; shake off excess. Heat oil in a wide frying pan over medium heat. Cook 2 fish at a time. Place fish in pan and cook until browned on each side, 3 to 4 minutes total. Transfer fish to a baking dish. Bake, uncovered, until center of the fish is opaque, about 10 minutes.

Prepare the sauce: In a saucepan heat chicken broth, ginger, soy, salt, and sugar to simmering over medium heat. Simmer, uncovered, for 5 minutes. Add brandy and simmer for 2 minutes. Add cornstarch mixture and cook, stirring, until sauce bubbles and thickens slightly. Correct seasoning with salt and pepper. When fish is done, transfer to a warm platter. Pour sauce over fish and serve.

Note: Unlike wild coho salmon which are large in size, farm-raised coho average 8 to 10 ounces (7 to 8 after boning) and make an attractive individual serving. Golden trout would also be a good choice to use here.

Pacific Snapper with Herb Butter-Caper Sauce

Makes 4 servings

*1 tablespoon chopped mixed fresh herbs: basil,
    thyme, and oregano*
1 teaspoon salt
1/2 teaspoon white pepper
4 snapper fillets (about 1 1/2 pounds)
All-purpose flour
1/4 cup clarified butter (page 109)
1/4 cup dry white wine
1/4 cup capers and juice
1 tablespoon lemon juice

Capers and herbs add zest to lean white-fleshed snapper. It is a perennial favorite with Fat City patrons.

In a small bowl combine herbs, salt, and pepper. Rub herbed salt on both sides of fillets. Dredge fish in flour; shake off excess.

Melt butter in a wide frying pan over medium-high heat. Add fish and cook, turning once, until fish is golden brown and center is opaque, 6 to 8 minutes. Transfer fish to a warm platter.

Reduce heat to medium. Add wine, capers, and lemon juice. Cook until sauce is reduced by half. Pour sauce over fish and serve.

Grilled Ahi Tuna with Papaya Relish

Makes 4 servings

Papaya Relish
1 papaya, peeled, seeded, and finely diced
1 1/2 tablespoons finely diced red onion
1 1/2 tablespoons finely diced red bell pepper
1 tablespoon lime juice
1 1/2 teaspoons sugar
1/8 teaspoon each ground cinnamon
  and cumin
Pinch each of ground ginger, mace,
  allspice, and white pepper
1 1/2 teaspoons olive oil
Salt

1/4 cup dry sherry
3 tablespoons soy sauce
2 teaspoons sugar
1 teaspoon white pepper
1 1/2 pounds ahi tuna fillet, cut about 1 inch
  thick, cut into 4 pieces

Golden papaya relish with a sweet-sour accent complements the buttery richness of fresh tuna. Tuna is best grilled over mesquite charcoal which burns hotter than fire produced by briquets. If you use briquets, add another minute to the cooking time, but no more. Tuna is one fish that can be served rare. Overcooking dries out the meat.

Prepare the relish: Combine all ingredients except salt in a glass bowl; add salt to taste. Cover and refrigerate for 8 hours.

In a small bowl, combine sherry, soy sauce, sugar, and pepper. Rub seasoning on both sides of fillets. Just before grilling fish, heat papaya relish over low heat.

Place fish on a well-greased grill 4 to 6 inches above a solid bed of hot coals. Cook, turning once, until outside of fish is almost crisp and center of fish just begins to turn opaque, 6 to 8 minutes. With a wide spatula, transfer fish to a warm platter. Spoon relish over one side of fish and serve.

Trout with Beer Brown Butter

Makes 4 servings

4 boneless trout (6 to 8 ounces each)
Salt and white pepper
All-purpose flour
1/4 cup clarified butter (page 109)
1 bottle (12 ounces) beer
1/2 teaspoon minced garlic
1 tablespoon chopped parsley
4 tablespoon cold butter, cut into 8 pieces

*T*he proliferation of new styles and brands of beer allows you to personalize this stylish presentation of trout. For the sauce, choose a beer that appeals to your taste and is not so strong as to overpower the delicate fish. At Fat City we use a medium-body ale.

Season trout inside and out with salt and pepper; fold trout closed. Dredge fish in flour; shake off excess.

Melt 2 tablespoons of the butter in a wide frying pan over medium-high heat. Place 2 fish in pan and cook until browned on both sides and center is opaque, 8 to 10 minutes total. Transfer fish to a warm platter and cover loosely to keep warm. Add the remaining 2 tablespoons butter to pan and cook the remaining fish. Transfer fish to serving platter.

Deglaze pan with beer, then add garlic. Cook over high heat until sauce is reduced by one-half. Add parsley. Reduce heat to low. Add butter, one piece at a time, stirring continuously. Add more butter just before previous piece has emulsified. Pour sauce over fish and serve.

Baked Sea Bass with Lemon-Butter Sauce

Makes 4 servings

4 sea bass fillets, 6 to 7 ounces each
3 tablespoons dry white wine
2 tablespoons lemon juice
1 teaspoon seasoned salt
1/2 teaspoon white pepper
2 tablespoons butter
1/4 cup chopped onion
1/4 cup chopped shallots
2 cloves garlic, minced
8 sprigs fresh dill, chopped

Lemon-Butter Sauce
6 tablespoons cold butter, cut into 6 pieces
1 tablespoon lemon juice
Salt and white pepper

At Fat City, sea bass is perfumed with fresh dill and baked, and the pan juices are transformed into a lemon-spiked butter sauce. You can substitute other firm-textured white fish fillets if you wish, such as snapper, rockfish, halibut, or ling cod.

Preheat oven to 400° F. Place fillets in a single layer in a glass baking dish. In a small bowl, mix wine, lemon juice, seasoned salt, and pepper. Pour over fish. Let fish marinate for 10 minutes, turning once.

Melt the 2 tablespoons butter in a small frying pan over medium heat. Add onion, shallots, and garlic. Cook until onion is soft. Spread onion mixture over fish. Sprinkle dill on top.

Bake fish, uncovered, until center of fish is opaque, 10 to 12 minutes. Lift fish from sauce with a slotted spatula and transfer to a warm serving platter.

Pour sauce into a medium frying pan. Cook until liquid is reduced by one-half. Over low heat, add the butter, one piece at a time. Whisking constantly, add more butter just before the previous piece has emulsified. Add the lemon juice and remove pan from heat. Taste; add salt and pepper. Pour sauce over fish and serve.

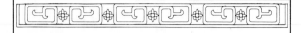

Asparagus Prawns with Black Bean Sauce

Makes 4 servings

Marinade
1 egg white, lightly beaten with a fork
1 tablespoon dry white wine
2 teaspoons cornstarch
1 teaspoon minced fresh ginger
1/2 teaspoon salt

1 pound large raw prawns, shelled and deveined
1 pound asparagus
4 tablespoons vegetable oil
1 small onion, cut in wedges, layers separated
1 tablespoon preserved black beans, rinsed, drained, and coarsely chopped
1 tablespoon minced garlic
1 teaspoon sugar
1/2 teaspoon salt
1/2 teaspoon sesame oil
1 teaspoon cornstarch mixed with 1/4 cup chicken broth
Steamed rice

*T*his classic stir-fry is a feast for both eyes and palate. In the heat of the wok, the prawns turn bright pink, and the green of asparagus brightens to the color of jade. Serve it with rice for an easy one-dish meal.

Combine marinade ingredients in a medium bowl. Add prawns and stir to coat. Cover and refrigerate for 1 hour. Snap off and discard the tough ends of asparagus; cut spears diagonally in 1 1/2-inch pieces.

Place a wok or wide frying pan over high heat until hot. Add 2 tablespoons of the vegetable oil, swirling to coat the sides. Add the prawns and stir-fry 2 to 3 minutes or until the prawns turn pink. Remove prawns from pan.

Add the remaining 2 tablespoons vegetable oil to pan. When oil is hot, add onion, black beans, and garlic. Stir-fry for 30 seconds. Add asparagus and stir once. Cover and cook for 2 minutes or until asparagus is crisp-tender. Add a spoonful of chicken broth or water if pan becomes dry. Return the prawns to the pan and add sugar, salt, and sesame oil. Add the cornstarch solution. Cook, stirring, until the sauce boils and thickens slightly. Serve with steamed rice.

Note: What's the difference between a shrimp and a prawn? The name depends on where you live. In some parts of the country large shrimp are called prawns, while smaller ones are called shrimp. In the South, all these tasty crustaceans are called shrimp. You can use shrimp and prawns interchangeably. Just be sure to cook the larger prawns a few seconds longer.

Lobster Soong

Makes 4 entree servings, 8 appetizer servings

Marinade
2 tablespoons water
1 tablespoon cornstarch
1 teaspoon sesame oil
1/4 teaspoon salt
1/8 teaspoon each white pepper and sugar
1/4 teaspoon minced fresh ginger and garlic

2 lobster tails (about 8 ounces each)
4 dried Chinese black mushrooms
2 to 3 tablespoons vegetable oil
1 1/2 Chinese sausages, diced (1/2 cup)
1/4 cup each diced carrot and celery
1/4 cup diced Chinese pea pods
1/4 cup each diced bamboo shoots and
*   water chestnuts*
3 green onions (white part only), chopped
2 tablespoons oyster sauce
1/2 teaspoon salt
1/4 cup chopped almonds

Hoisin sauce
About 2 dozen iceberg lettuce cups, washed,
*   drained, and chilled*

Chinese New Years is the time we pull out all stops at California Fats to celebrate with traditional foods. Lobster Soong brings double good luck: lobster, the dragon shrimp, means prosperity, and lettuce prophesies wealth. The contrast of lobster soong is appealing. Crisp chilled lettuce cups hold the hot stir-fried mixture.

Combine marinade ingredients in a medium bowl. Remove lobster meat from shells and dice. Add lobster to marinade; stir to coat. Refrigerate, covered, for 1 hour. Soak mushrooms in warm water to cover for 30 minutes; drain. Cut off stems; dice the caps.

Place a wok or wide frying pan over high heat until hot. Add 2 tablespoons of the oil, swirling to coat pan sides. Add the lobster and stir-fry for 1 minute or until lobster meat turns opaque. Remove lobster from pan. Add sausage, carrot, and celery. Stir-fry for 1 minute. Add mushrooms, pea pods, bamboo shoots, water chestnuts, and green onions; add another tablespoon of oil if food sticks to pan. Add oyster sauce and salt. Stir-fry for 1 minute. Return lobster to pan. Add almonds and mix well. Place on a warm serving platter.

Present lobster at the table with a bowl of hoisin sauce and lettuce cups. To eat, spread a little hoisin sauce on a lettuce cup, spoon in some lobster, wrap up in lettuce, and eat out of hand.

Note: This dish calls for a lot of chopping; each piece should be cut in 1/8-inch dice. A 1/4-inch dice is not considered as visually appealing, but will taste marvelous. No matter what size dice, all ingredients should be the same size to ensure even cooking.

Butterflied Sesame Shrimp

Makes 4 servings

1 pound medium raw shrimp
1/4 cup water chestnuts
1/3 pound small raw shrimp, shelled
    and deveined
1/4 pound lean ground pork
2 tablespoons soy sauce
1/2 teaspoon salt
1/2 teaspoon sugar
About 1/2 cup sesame seeds
Vegetable oil for deep-fat frying
Hot mustard sauce

These unusual shrimp are as welcomed as an appetizer as they are in the role of an entree. You can prepare and refrigerate the shrimp up to 4 hours ahead of serving, but for a juicy texture and crisp coating, deep-fry them just before serving.

Shell medium shrimp, leaving tail shells on. With a sharp knife, cut deep into vein line of each shrimp, over halfway through meat. Press each shrimp firmly open so it resembles a butterfly. Rinse out sand veins, pat shrimp dry with paper towels, and set aside.

In a food processor, coarsely chop water chestnuts. Add small shrimp, pork, soy sauce, salt, and sugar. Process to make a rough paste. Using about 2 tablespoons of shrimp paste for each, press a thin layer of paste on both sides of each butterflied shrimp; leave tail section clean. Coat the wrapped shrimp with sesame seeds.

In a wok or deep heavy pan, pour oil to a depth of 2 inches. Heat oil to 350° F over medium-high heat. Slide 3 or 4 shrimp into oil and cook for 3 or 4 minutes or until golden brown. Remove with a slotted spoon and drain on paper towels. Keep shrimp warm in a 200° F oven while cooking the rest. Serve with mustard sauce for dipping.

Note: Hot mustard sauce is easily made. Blend equal parts of dry mustard powder with water until smooth.

Shrimp Nori

Makes 4 entree servings, 8 appetizer servings

Shrimp Paste
1/2 pound small raw shrimp, shelled and deveined
2 ounces boneless skinless chicken breast,
    diced (1/4 cup)
2 ounces lean ground pork (1/4 cup)
1/4 cup water chestnuts, chopped
2 tablespoons chopped almonds
1 tablespoon chopped cilantro
    (Chinese parsley)
1 teaspoon minced garlic
1 teaspoon minced fresh ginger
1 green onion and top, chopped
1 teaspoon soy sauce
1 teaspoon salt
1/2 teaspoon sugar

8 sheets plain toasted nori
1 egg, lightly beaten
Vegetable oil for deep-fat frying

Norimaki, the Japanese name for rolled sushi, was the starting point for this dish. Using nori (seaweed) for the wrapper is traditional, but in place of a rice-based filling, I use a paste of shrimp, chicken, and pork. When the rolls are deep-fried, the filling turns pink and the nori wrapper becomes extra crisp and glossy.

Prepare shrimp paste: Combine all paste ingredients in a food processor and process to make a coarse paste. With scissors, cut nori in roughly 4-inch squares. To make each, place 1 tablespoon of shrimp paste across center of a nori square. Roll nori around filling and overlap edges to form a closed cylinder. Ends of nori should remain open and shrimp paste should extend to the ends. Brush both ends of each roll with beaten egg to seal.

In a wok or deep heavy pan, pour oil to a depth of about 2 inches. Heat oil to 360° F over medium-high heat. Slide 4 or 5 rolls into oil and cook for 4 to 5 minutes or until filling at ends turns pink. Remove with a slotted spoon and drain on paper towels. Repeat until all rolls are cooked. Trim ends of rolls, then cut rolls into 1/2 inch slices. Stand slices on serving platter so filling shows. Serve warm.

Note: Nori is available in Asian markets. Most packages contain 8 sheets, each about 8 inches square. For best flavor, look for a label that says toasted nori. To store leftover nori, place in an airtight container and store in a cool dry place, or to retain maximum freshness, freeze.

Crab Cakes with Chile-Cream Sauce

Makes 4 entree servings, 8 appetizer servings

Chile-Cream Sauce
2 dried red California or New Mexico chiles
1 tablespoon olive oil
2 cloves garlic
1/4 cup oyster sauce
1 teaspoon chile paste
Pinch of saffron
1 cup heavy cream

1 pound cooked crab meat, flaked
1/2 pound sweet potato, peeled and finely
   shredded
1/2 pound zucchini, finely shredded, squeezed
   to extract all moisture
2 tablespoons minced parsley
1 tablespoon minced garlic
1 tablespoon minced shallot
2 teaspoons ground cumin
1 teaspoon salt
1 teaspoon black pepper
1/2 teaspoon cayenne
2 eggs, lightly beaten
1/2 cup all-purpose flour
Vegetable oil

At California Fats we look forward to the opening of crab season. It signals a return of spicy crab cakes on our menu. The patties are juicy within, crisp on the outside, and topped with a silky chile sauce. If you wish to serve these as an appetizer, make bite-size crab cakes and pass the chile-cream sauce in a bowl for dipping.

Prepare the sauce: Remove and discard seeds and stems from chiles. Place chiles in a bowl, cover with boiling water, and let stand until soft, about 20 minutes; drain. In a blender, puree chiles, olive oil, garlic, oyster sauce, chili paste, and saffron. Place chile mixture in a small pan and stir in cream. Cook over low heat, stirring frequently, until sauce has thickened to heavy cream consistency. Remove pan from heat and strain sauce through a fine sieve.

In a large bowl, combine crab, sweet potato, zucchini, parsley, garlic, shallot, cumin, salt, pepper, cayenne, and eggs; mix well. Sprinkle in flour and stir until evenly blended. The mixture should be moist but not runny. Shape into 8 patties, each about 1/4 inch thick.

In a wide frying pan, pour oil to a depth of 1/4 inch and place over medium-high heat. When oil is hot, place crab cakes in pan. Cook, turning once, until sweet potato is cooked and crab cakes are golden brown, 6 to 8 minutes total. Drain on paper towels. Reheat chile-cream sauce, spoon over crab cakes, and serve.

Meats

Immigrant's Beef

Fat City Pepper Steak

Boneless Short Ribs

Drunk Steak

Spicy Teriyaki Kebabs

Irish Steak

Lemongrass Steak

Herbed Standing Rib Roast

Beef Cabernet

Duke Burger

Old Sacramento Chili

Beef and Brie Enchiladas

Pork Chops with Hoisin-Apple Relish

Plum-Glazed Pork Ribs

Barbecued Pork Loin

Barbecued Lamb Kebabs

Veal in Madeira Wine Sauce

Grilled Venison Steak

Immigrant's Beef

Makes 4 servings

1 large (1 1/2 to 2 pounds) flank steak
1/4 cup soy sauce
1/4 cup vegetable oil
1 tablespoon brandy
1 tablespoon minced garlic
1 tablespoon minced fresh ginger
1/4 teaspoon sesame oil
2 teaspoons cornstarch
24 trimmed asparagus spears or
    4 to 6 broccoli spears

When China Camp opened its door, the menu featured this entree patterned after a dish cooked by early Chinese immigrants. At California Fats, we've retained the zesty flavor of the meat but updated the presentation: tender medallions of flank steak are served over fresh seasonal vegetables.

Trim fat from meat. Cut flank steak lengthwise into 3-inch wide strips; cut diagonally across the grain to make 2 inch wide pieces. When cutting, hold knife at an angle so each piece of meat is about 1/4 inch thick. In a medium bowl, combine soy sauce, vegetable oil, brandy, garlic, ginger, sesame oil, and cornstarch. Add beef and stir to coat. Cover and refrigerate for at least 2 hours or overnight.

Just before cooking meat, blanch asparagus or broccoli in boiling salted water for 3 minutes or until barely tender. Drain, rinse with cold water, and drain again; arrange on a serving platter.

Heat a wide heavy frying pan over high heat; grease lightly. Cook meat in pan, turning once, until brown on both sides, about 2 minutes total. Place meat over asparagus or broccoli and serve.

Slicing and Mincing Ginger

We use a great deal of ginger in our cooking and with a continuous fresh suppply, the skin is thin, never wrinkled and dry. When a dish calls for minced ginger, I smash slices of unpeeled ginger with a cleaver or chef's knife, then chop the slices very finely. When a dish calls for slivers or fine julienne ginger strips, I peel the ginger. This is important for visual appeal. If you work with ginger that has a dry, tough skin, peel it with a paring knife before mincing or slicing.

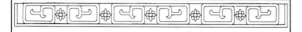

Fat City Pepper Steak

Makes 4 servings

1/4 cup cracked black pepper
1 teaspoon salt
4 New York steaks (10 to 12 ounces each), cut
    1 1/2 inches thick
1/4 cup clarified butter
1/4 cup brandy
1 cup beef broth
1 cup heavy cream
4 teaspoons Dijon mustard
4 teaspoons green peppercorns with brine

At Fat City our customers look forward to splurging with a generously cut steak. Twelve ounces of meat is our standard portion for pepper steak. If you prefer to serve small steaks, or if you are cooking for two, cut the recipe in half. Any cut of tender boneless beef takes well to this treatment. Just be sure to adjust the cooking time according to the thickness of the meat.

In a small bowl, combine pepper and salt. Press mixture on both sides of steaks. Melt butter in a wide heavy frying pan over medium heat. Place steaks in pan and cook until meat is browned on both sides and done to your liking, 4 to 5 minutes on each side for rare. Pour brandy around the steaks. Cook until alcohol evaporates. Transfer steaks to a warm serving platter.

Add broth, cream and mustard to pan drippings; whisk to blend. Boil rapidly over high heat until sauce is slightly thickened and large shiny bubbles form. Stir in green peppercorns. Pour sauce over steaks and serve.

Clarified Butter

For the quick sautees used in restaurant cooking, clarified butter is an ideal cooking fat. Clarifying removes the milk protein and salt found naturally in butter. If left in, this white sediment of casein and salt burns easily and could impart a harsh flavor.

To clarify butter, melt 1 cup butter in a small pan over low heat. As the milky foam rises, skim it off and discard it. Pour off the clear, golden melted butter, discarding the white milk solids at the bottom of the pan. This makes about 3/4 cup clarified butter. Store it in the refrigerator for up to 2 weeks.

Boneless Short Ribs

Makes 4 servings

2 teaspoons sesame seeds
1 cup chopped, peeled, cored Bartlett pear
1 cup chopped onion
1 tablespoon minced garlic
1/2 cup chopped green onions and tops
2 tablespoons sugar
1 teaspoon black pepper
1/4 cup water
1/4 cup soy sauce
2 tablespoons pear liqueur
2 pounds Korean-style boneless beef short ribs

*E*nglish-cut short ribs are a very flavorful cut of meat, but with with a high ratio of bone to meat they are messy to eat. At California Fats, we buy Korean-style short ribs which have been sawed across the bone, then trim the tiny rib bones at the end to make tender boneless strips of meat. In the typical Korean marinade, Asian pear is used for sweetness. For a more intense fruity flavor, I developed this marinade using sweet Barlett pears and pear liqueur.

Toast sesame seeds in a dry frying pan over medium heat, shaking pan frequently, until fragrant and golden, 2 to 3 minutes. Coarsely crush seeds with a mortar and pestle. Place in a large bowl. Add pear, onion, garlic, green onions, sugar, pepper, water, soy sauce, and liqueur. Mix well. Add meat, turning to coat both sides. Cover and refrigerate overnight; turn once or twice during marinating.

Lift meat from marinade and drain briefly. Heat a wide heavy frying pan over high heat; grease lightly. Cook meat, turning once, until done to your liking, 6 minutes total for medium-rare.

Note: If you cannot find Korean-style beef short ribs, look for them by their other name, flanken ribs. Each strip of meat is about 6 inches long and 1/4 inch thick. Trim the tiny rib bones at the end or leave them in. Either way, the meat tastes marvelous.

Drunk Steak

Makes 4 to 8 servings

4 tablespoons minced garlic
4 tablespoons minced fresh ginger
1/4 cup brandy
2 tablespoons soy sauce
1 teaspoon sugar
4 New York steaks or club steaks (10 to 12
*   ounces each), cut 1 inch thick*
2 tablespoons vegetable oil
2 tablespoons beef broth

When it first appeared on the menu, the name of this dish made an instant hit with California Fats' clientele. Curiosity and a sense of adventure generated initial orders. Satisfying taste has guaranteed a multitude of repeat orders.

In a bowl combine 2 tablespoons of the garlic with the ginger, brandy, soy sauce, and the sugar. Add steaks, turning to coat both sides. Cover and refrigerate 1 to 2 hours; turn meat once or twice during marinating.

Lift steaks from marinade and drain briefly. Heat oil in a wide heavy frying pan over high heat. Place steaks in pan and brown for 2 minutes on each side. Turn heat to medium-high and continue cooking until meat is done to your liking (cut to test), 3 to 4 minutes for medium-rare. Pour 2 tablespoons of the brandy around steaks. Cook until alcohol evaporates. Transfer steaks to a warm serving platter.

Add the remaining 2 tablespoons brandy to pan and stir to scrape up browned bits. Add the remaining 2 tablespoons garlic and 2 tablespoons ginger. Cook for 30 seconds. Add beef broth. Stir once or twice, bring sauce to a boil, then pour sauce over steaks.

Spicy Teriyaki Kebabs

Makes 6 to 8 servings

2/3 cup soy sauce
2/3 cup lime juice
2 teaspoons chopped fresh mint
1 clove garlic, minced
4 teaspoons sugar
1 to 1 1/2 teaspoons crushed dried red chiles
2 pounds top sirloin steak, cut into
    1 1/2-inch cubes
1 green bell pepper, seeded and cut into
    1 1/2-inch squares
1 red bell pepper, seeded and cut into
    1 1/2-inch squares
2 medium onions, cut into wedges

*S*oy sauce is the common denominator in teriyaki sauce. In its home country, Japan, teriyaki sauce is spiked with sake and sweetened with sugar and sweet rice wine. My version has Southeast Asian overtones. Fresh lime juice and mint gives it a clean fresh taste, crushed chiles provide the heat.

In a bowl, combine soy sauce, lime juice, mint, garlic, sugar, and chiles. Add the meat, turning to coat all sides. Cover and refrigerate 2 to 3 hours; turn meat once or twice during marinating.

Lift meat from marinade and drain briefly, reserving marinade. On long metal skewers, alternately thread meat cubes, bell pepper pieces, and onion wedges. Place skewers on a lightly greased grill above a solid bed of glowing coals. Cook, turning skewers often and basting occasionally with mariande, 15 to 18 minutes or until meat is browned on all sides and done to your liking (cut meat to test).

Irish Steak

Makes 4 servings

1 1/2 pounds beef tenderloin or top sirloin
4 tablespoons olive oil
4 tablespoons Irish whiskey
2 tablespoons minced shallot
2 cloves garlic, minced
Salt and pepper
1/2 pound white onions, sliced tip to tip
1 pound mushrooms, sliced

*F*at City regulars look forward to specials we create for holiday menus. To toast Saint Patrick's Day, we offer this zingy steak. It's wonderful accompanied with roasted red thin-skinned potatoes and a savory slaw.

Cut meat across the grain to make 12 medallions, each 2 inches by 3 inches by 1/2 inch thick. In a medium bowl, combine 2 tablespoons of the oil with 2 tablespoons of the whiskey, shallot, and garlic. Add the meat, turning to coat all sides. Cover and refrigerate overnight; turn once or twice during marinating.

Heat the remaining 2 tablespoons oil in a wide heavy frying pan over high heat. Place medallions in pan and cook until meat is browned on both sides, 2 minutes on each side. Season meat with salt and pepper to taste; remove meat from pan.

Add onions and mushrooms to pan. Cook until onions are soft and pan juices have evaporated. Return meat to pan. Pour the remaining 2 tablespoons whiskey around meat. Cook until alcohol evaporates. Place medallions on a warm serving platter. Spoon onion and mushrooms over the top.

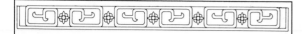

Lemongrass Steak

Makes 6 to 8 servings

3 stalks lemongrass
1/4 cup thinly sliced chives
1 clove garlic, minced
1 tablespoon olive oil
1 teaspoon Thai chili paste
1 bonelesss top sirloin steak or top round steak
(sometimes called London broil), cut
2 inches thick (2 to 2 1/2 pounds)
Salt and pepper

*F*or a dinner in a hurry, you can pan-broil this mouth-watering steak in a thin film of oil, as we do at California Fats, or if you prefer, grill it on the barbecue. The flavor secret is the lemongrass-chili paste mixture that is spread on top after the meat is cooked.

Use only the bottom 6 inches of lemongrass. Discard dried tough outer stalks; thinly slice tender core. In a mini food processor, combine lemongrass, chives, garlic, oil, and chili paste. Process to make a rough paste; set aside.

Place steak in a lightly greased, heavy frying pan over medium heat or place on a lightly greased grill 4 to 6 inches above a solid bed of glowing coals. Cook, turning once, for 12 to 15 minutes on each side for rare or until done to your liking (cut to test). Spread lemongrass paste on top of steak. Salt and pepper to taste. Cut meat across the grain in thin slanting slices.

Note: When I first experimented with Southeast Asian seasonings, it was disappointing to find fresh lemongrass only available on an irregular basis. Now widely available, it is one of my favorite herbs any time I want to give a dish—from salad to steak— an intriguing lemony flavor. To store, wrap lemongrass in a paper towel, place in a plastic bag, and refrigerate for up to 2 weeks. Freeze for longer storage.

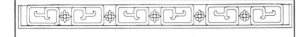

Herbed Standing Rib Roast

Makes 10 to 12 servings

*1/2 cup chopped mixed fresh herbs: rosemary,
    thyme, oregano, and marjoram*
1/2 cup cracked black pepper
6 to 8-pound standing rib beef roast
Cheesecloth
1 cup rock salt
1 cup beef broth
1 tablespoon brandy
Horseradish cream (optional)

We serve this king of roasts for holiday meals and special parties as an interesting alternative to turkey. The meat is roasted under a layer of rock salt, pepper, and herbs. Scraped off before serving, the crusty coating helps seal in the meat juices. If an excess of salt spills on the cutting board as you scrape off the coating, wipe the board clean before slicing the meat.

Preheat oven to 425° F. In a small bowl, combine herbs and pepper. Cut off fat cap from roast in one piece and reserve. Rub herb mixture on all sides of meat. Stand roast on a double thickness of cheesecloth large enough to wrap around meat. Lay fat cap on top of meat. Pat rock salt all over roast. Wrap cheesecloth around meat. Insert a meat thermometer into thickest portion of meat without touching bone

Place roast, fat side up, on a rack on a shallow baking pan. Roast, uncovered, for 20 minutes. Reduce oven to 325° F. Continue to roast 1 1/4 to 1 1/2 hours for rare to medium-rare (meat thermometer will register 130°) or until done to your liking. Internal temperature of meat will rise 5 to 10 degrees after meat is removed from the oven. Transfer roast to a cutting board and let stand 10 to 15 minutes. Remove cheesecloth and scrape off rock salt. Slice to desired thickness and arrange on a serving platter.

While roast is resting, pour pan juices into a small pan; skim fat. Add broth and brandy; heat until simmering. Serve roast with sauce and, if desired, horseradish cream.

Horseradish Cream

Fold freshly grated horseradish to taste into 1 1/2 cups whipped cream (1/2 cup cream before whipping). If you like, add a teaspoon of Dijon mustard.

Beef Cabernet

Makes 6 servings

1/4 pound bacon, diced
1/4 cup all-purpose flour
1 teaspoon salt
1/2 teaspoon pepper
1 teaspoon mild Hungarian paprika
2 1/2 pounds boneless beef chuck, cut into
    1-inch cubes
1 medium carrot, cut in 1/2-inch dice
1 stalk celery, cut in 1/2-inch dice
1 large onion, cut in 1/2-inch dice
2 cups Cabernet Sauvignon wine
1 cup beef broth
1 tablespoon tomato paste
Spice bag: 1 bay leaf, 3 cloves crushed garlic,
    4 sprigs parsley, 4 sprigs fresh thyme, and
    1 teaspoon whole black peppers (tied to-
    gether in cheesecloth)
1 tablespoon olive oil
1 cup small whole mushrooms
1 cup peeled small whole onions (3/4 to 1 inch
    diameter)
1 cup each each diced green and yellow zucchini
    and yellow crookneck squash, cut in
    1-inch chunks

Wine, beef, onions, and mushrooms are the essense of *boeuf bourguignon*, a savory stew from the Burgundy region of France. To give a California twist to this traditional dish, I use a full-bodied Napa Valley cabernet wine and add a trio of bright summer squashes. For a easy company meal, serve Beef Cabernet over rice. Complete the meal with crisp green salad greens dressed with oil and vinegar, and for dessert, perhaps Pumpkin Hazelnut Cake, (page 145).

In a wide frying pan, cook bacon over medium heat until crisp. Remove from pan with a slotted spoon and place in a 5-quart kettle. On a plate combine flour, salt, pepper, and paprika. Dredge meat in flour mixture, shaking off excess. Over medium-high heat, cook meat, a portion at a time, in bacon drippings until browned on all sides. Transfer meat to kettle with bacon. Add carrot, celery, and onion to pan. Cook until onion is soft, 5 to 7 minutes. Place vegetables in kettle with meat. Add wine to frying pan, scrape any browned bits on bottom of pan, then pour over meat. To the meat add broth, tomato paste, and spice bag. Bring to a boil; cover, reduce heat, and simmer until meat is tender when pierced, 1 to 1 1/4 hours.

Meanwhile heat oil in a wide frying pan over medium-high heat. Add mushrooms, onions, and squashes. Cook, stirring frequently, until vegetables are lightly browned. When meat is cooked, stir in mushroom mixture; cover and simmer until vegetables are just tender when pierced, 10 to 15 minutes. Remove spice bag and skim fat from sauce before serving.

Duke Burger

Makes 6 servings

1 pound lean ground lamb
1 pound lean ground beef
1/3 chopped onion
1/3 cup coarsely chopped cilantro
    (Chinese parsley)
1/3 cup tomato sauce
1/4 cup cooked rice
1 teaspoon minced garlic
1 teaspoon chopped fresh mint
1 teaspoon seasoned salt
1/8 teaspoon each pepper, cayenne, and
    ground cinnamon
6 sesame seed hamburger buns,
    split and toasted
6 slices tomato
6 canned grape leaves, rinsed (to remove
    brine) and drained
Condiments: Mustard, catsup, sliced pickles,
    sliced onion

We are proud of having a long history of counting Sacramento politicians among our regular clientele, and on occasion, politics have influenced our menus! We created this recipe when George Deukmejian was inaugurated as governor in California in 1983. The seasonings in the meat patty pay homage to his Greek ancestry. We served it, American style, with mustard, catsup, pickles, onions—the works.

Crumble ground meats into a large bowl. Add onion, cilantro, tomato sauce, rice, garlic, mint, seasoned salt, pepper, cayenne, and cinnamon; mix well. Divide mixture into 6 equal portions; lightly shape each portion into a patty about 1 inch thick.

Place patties on a lightly greased grill 4 to 6 inches above a solid bed of glowing coals. Cook, turning once, for 3 to 4 minutes on each side for rare or until done to you liking (cut to test). Place a tomato slice and a grape leaf inside of each bun, then top with a meat patty. Serve with condiments as desired.

Old Sacramento Chili

Makes 6 servings

1 or 2 dried red California or New Mexico chiles
1/4 pound bacon, diced
2 1/2 pounds boneless beef chuck, fat trimmed, cut in 1/4 inch dice
1 tablespoon salt
1 1/2 tablespoons black pepper
2 medium onions, chopped
3 cloves garlic, minced
1/4 cup chili powder
2 tablespoons cumin seeds
2 tablespoons dried oregano
1/2 teaspoon cayenne
4 large tomatoes, peeled and chopped
1 cup tomato juice
1 can (7 ounces) diced green chiles
1/4 cup tomato paste
3/4 teaspoon sugar
2 to 3 cups cooked red, pinto, or pink beans, drained
Chopped onion
Shredded Cheddar cheese

*F*ollowing official contest rules, our "bowl of red" did not contain beans when it was presented to judges in the Old Sacramento chili cook-off (we won second prize), but for the public tasting we added red beans— the way I like my chili. I don't believe an official standard for chili hotness exists, but on a scale of 1 for mild to 10 for searingly hot, I would rate ours between 5 and 7. The chili calls for meat cut in 1/4-inch dice. You can speed up the dicing by partially freezing the meat first. If you don't have the patience for this meticulous cutting, use coarsely ground meat (sometimes called chili grind).

Wash dried chiles; remove stems and seeds. Place in a small pan with water to cover. Cover and simmer 20 minutes or until chiles are very soft. In a blender, process chiles with 1 or 2 tablespoons of the water until pureed; reserve.

In a wide frying pan, cook bacon over medium heat until crisp. Remove from pan with a slotted spoon and set aside; discard half of drippings. In batches, brown meat in drippings over high heat. As each portion is browned, transfer to a 5-quart pot. Add salt and pepper to meat. Add onions and garlic to remaining pan drippings. Cook, stirring often, over medium heat until onions are soft, about 10 minutes. Add chili powder, cumin seeds, oregano, and cayenne. Cook for 1 minute. Add onion mixture to meat.

To the meat, add reserved chiles, tomatoes, tomato juice, green chiles, tomato paste, and sugar. Bring to a boil; reduce heat, cover, and simmer for 1 1/2 hours or until meat is very tender. Stir in beans and heat through. Ladle into bowls and garnish each serving with onion and cheese.

Note: Cooking beans is easy and requires little attention, but you need to plan ahead because all dried beans require presoaking. Rinse and sort beans, then soak them by one of the following methods:

Quick soaking. Place 1 pound dried beans in a large pot with 2 quarts hot water. Heat to boiling and cook for 2 minutes. Turn off heat. Cover and let stand for 1 hour. Drain; discard water.

Long soaking. Place 1 pound dried beans in a large pot with 2 quarts cold water. Soak overnight. Drain; discard water.

To cook beans. After draining soaked beans, add 2 quarts fresh water. Bring to a boil; reduce heat and simmer, with lid ajar, until beans are tender, 1 to 2 hours, depending on kind of beans used. When beans are tender, add salt to taste. Beans double in size during cooking; 1 pound dry beans yield about 4 cups cooked beans.

Chili or Chile?

When you see chili spelled with an "i", this refers to a bowl of chili or the seasoning, chili powder, made from chile peppers, cumin, oregano, salt, and garlic. Chile spelled with an "e" refers to powder, mild or hot, made from pure ground chiles. For our championship dish, we used dried red chiles, chili powder, and canned green chiles.

Beef and Brie Enchiladas

Makes 4 servings

Marinade
1 1/2 tablespoons lemon juice
2 teaspoons lime juice
2 tablespoons chopped onion
1 clove garlic, minced
1/2 serrano chile, minced with seeds
2 tablespoons each olive oil and vegetable oil
1/2 teaspoon ground cumin
1/4 teaspoon salt
1/8 teaspoon each ground cinnamon, oregano,
    and black pepper

1 1/2 pounds boneless beef chuck,
    fat trimmed, cut into 1-inch cubes
2 tablespoons vegetable oil
3 cups beef consomme
8 corn tortillas, 6 inches in diamter
8 ounces brie cheese, cut into 16 strips
3/4 cup tomatillo salsa or regular salsa

In these succulent enchiladas, shredded beef is wrapped up with creamy brie cheese and green salsa. At Fat City, this specialty is served with black beans, guacamole, and sour cream, and gilded with sliced green onions and dollops of green and red salsa.

In a medium bowl, combine marinade ingredients. Add beef and stir to coat. Refrigerate, covered, overnight. Heat the 2 tablespoons oil in a 5-quart kettle over medium-high heat. Add meat, half at a time, and cook until browned on all sides. Add consomme to meat and heat to simmering. Cover and bake in a 350° F oven for 1 hour or until meat is very tender. Let meat cool slightly, then lift from pan juices. Using 2 forks, shred meat.

Heat a nonstick frying pan over medium-high heat. Place 1 tortilla in pan; cook 15 seconds on each side or until soft. Remove tortilla from pan and place 1 strip of brie, 2 tablespoons of meat, and 1 tablespoon of salsa across center of tortilla; roll to enclose. Place enchilada, seam side down, in a shallow baking pan. Repeat until all tortillas are filled. Top with the remaining 1/4 cup salsa. Lay a strip of brie lengthwise on each enchilada. Bake, uncovered, in a 350° F oven 5 to 7 minutes or until heated through.

Note: We make enchiladas to order so they heat in minutes. If you assemble them ahead of time, reserve the strips of brie which go on top. Bake enchiladas, covered, 20 minutes. Uncover, top with brie, and continue baking 5 minutes or until cheese is melted.

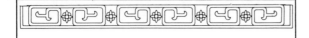

Pork Chops with Hoisin-Apple Relish

Makes 4 to 8 servings

Hoisin-Apple Relish
2 red-skinned apples with peel on, cored
    and diced
2 tablespoons finely chopped red bell pepper
1 shallot, finely chopped
1 tablespoon chopped fresh pineapple sage or
    regular sage
2 serrano chiles, seeded and finely chopped
2 tablespoons hoisin sauce
2 tablespoons lime juice
2 teaspoons lemon juice
1/2 teaspoon salt
1/4 teaspoon white pepper
1/8 teaspoon ground cumin

1/4 cup chopped fresh pineapple sage or
    regular sage
2 tablespoons olive oil
2 tablespoons lime juice
1 teaspoon salt
1/2 teaspoon black pepper
8 boneless center-cut pork loin chops, 3/4 to
    1 inch thick (2 pounds total)
1 tablespoon vegetable oil

*E*ast-west flavors accent these tender pork chops. Chinese hoisin sauce lends a sweet, spicy flavor. Cumin and sage give warm earthy overtones. At a specialty produce fair, I discovered pineapple sage which we now use in this dish. If you are a gardener, you might want to save space in your herb garden to grow this distinctive variety of sage.

Prepare the relish: Combine all ingredients in a bowl. Cover and refrigerate for at least 1 hour or as long as overnight.

In a medium bowl, combine sage, olive oil, lime juice, salt, and pepper. Add the meat, turning to coat all sides. Cover and refrigerate for 2 hours; turn meat once or twice during marinating.

Lift meat from marinade, drain briefly, and pat dry with paper towels. Heat vegetable oil in a wide frying pan over medium heat. Add meat and cook, turning occasionally, 10 to 12 minutes or until still moist and white in center (cut to test). Serve chops with relish.

Note: In Chinese cooking, hoisin sauce is an all-purpose sauce used both as a table condiment and a seasoning ingredient. It's wonderful with pork, poultry, and shellfish. Refrigerate hoisin sauce after opening the can or bottle. It will keep indefinitely.

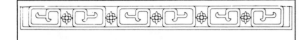

Plum-Glazed Pork Ribs

Makes 6 to 8 servings

Plum Glaze
3/4 pound fresh purple plums, pitted and
    coarsely chopped
1 cup dry red wine or dry port wine
1/4 pound bacon, finely diced
2 tablespoons olive oil
1 large onion, finely diced
1 tablespoon minced garlic
3/4 cup chicken broth
1/4 cup molasses
1/4 cup tomato paste
2 tablespoons dry mustard
2 tablespoons sugar
2 tablespoons honey
2 tablespoons hoisin sauce
2 tablespoons red wine vinegar
1/2 teaspoon each salt and pepper
2 tablespoons lemon juice

2 sides pork spareribs (6 to 8 pounds total),
    cut in 4 pieces

*F*inger-lickin' good, this is an ideal entree to serve on a warm summer evening. Take a tip from Asian food service: pass a basket of hot washcloths for hand wiping before serving dessert.

Prepare the glaze: In a small stainless steel pan, simmer plums in wine, uncovered, about 10 minutes or until plums are tender. Smoothly puree plums and wine in a blender or food processor; set aside.

In a 3-quart pan, cook bacon over medium heat until crisp. Remove with a slotted spoon and set aside; discard drippings. Heat olive oil in pan. Add onion and garlic and cook 6 to 8 minutes or until onion is soft. Add chicken broth, molasses, tomato paste, dry mustard, sugar, honey, hoisin sauce, wine vinegar, salt, and pepper. Stir in pureed plums and bacon. Bring to a boil; reduce heat and simmer, covered, for 1 hour or until glaze thickens. Stir frequently as glaze thickens. Stir in lemon juice, remove from heat, and set aside.

Place ribs in a large deep kettle with enough boiling water to cover them completely. Reduce heat and simmer for 15 minutes; drain. Brush ribs generously with glaze.

Bank low-glowing coals on each side of fire grill and place a metal drip pan in center. Place grill 4 to 6 inches above drip pan; lightly grease grill. Place ribs directly over drip pan. Cover barbecue and adjust dampers according to manufacturer's directions.

Cook, turning occasionally and basting several times with glaze, for 1 hour or until meat is very tender and can easily separate from the bone. Cut into serving-size pieces and serve.

Barbecued Pork Loin

Makes 6 to 8 servings

1/2 cup catsup
1/4 cup hoisin sauce
2 tablespoons brandy
2 teaspoons oyster sauce
1/2 cup sugar
2 tablespoons minced garlic
1 teaspoon salt
1 boneless pork loin, 2 1/2 to 3 pounds

*H*ere is a slightly different slant on barbecued pork, more lean and garlicky than traditional Chinese *char siu*. It makes an impressive sight as it spit-roasts to a crusty brown color. We serve it as an entree and use it to garnish noodle and rice dishes.

In a wide shallow bowl combine catsup, hoisin sauce, brandy, oyster sauce, sugar, garlic, and salt. Add pork and turns to coat all sides. Cover and refrigerate for 4 hours or overnight.

Arrange a solid bed of low-glowing coals in fire grill. Rub most of marinade off meat and reserve. Run spit through the center of roast and secure meat with spit forks. Position spit on barbecue and start motor. Cook, brushing occasionally during the last 30 minutes with reserved marinade, 45 minutes to 1 hour or until meat thermometer inserted in thickest portion registers 170° F. Remove meat from grill and allow to rest 10 minutes before carving. Internal temperature of meat will rise to 180° F.

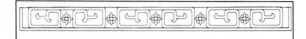

Barbecued Lamb Kebabs

Makes 6 servings

Marinade
1 cup light (thin) soy sauce
1/4 cup lime juice
1 tablespoon minced fresh mint
1 tablespoon minced garlic
1 tablespoon sugar
1 teaspoon crushed dried red chiles
1/2 teaspoon salt

2 pounds boneless lamb (cut from leg), fat trimmed, cut into 1 1/2-inch cubes
2 large green bell peppers, seeded and cut into 1 1/2-inch squares
2 onions, cut into 1 1/2-inch squares

*S*kewered lamb is a classic use of lamb in barbecue cooking, but this marinade is far from traditional. The lime juice-mint-garlic-chile combination is similar to one used by Thai and Malaysian cooks who hawk tiny meat skewers from push carts. Rice pilaf makes an excellent accompaniment, as does spicy fruit chutney.

In a medium bowl, combine marinade ingredients. Add lamb and stir to coat. Cover and refrigerate for 2 to 4 hours; turn meat one or twice during marinating.

Lift meat from marinade and drain briefly, reserving marinade. On long metal skewers, alternately thread meat cubes, bell pepper pieces, and onion squares. Place skewers on a lightly greased grill above a solid bed of glowing coals. Cook, turning skewers often and basting occasionally with marinade, 20 to 25 minutes or until lamb is well browned on all sides but still pink in center when cut.

Note: If you enjoy a smoky flavor, use soaked hickory chips or freshly cut wood on the fire.

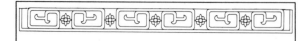

Veal in Madeira Wine Sauce

Makes 4 servings

1 pound boneless veal cutlets, cut 1/3 inch thick
1/4 cup all-purpose flour
1/2 teaspoon salt
1/8 teaspoon pepper
1/4 cup olive oil
1/4 cup Madeira wine
3/4 pound oyster mushrooms, sliced
2 teaspoons minced garlic
2 teaspoons minced shallot
1/2 cup beef broth
1/4 cup heavy cream

*T*his veal is cooked by the scaloppine technique: a little pounding to tenderize the meat and a short saute in a frying pan. We smother the cutlets with oyster mushrooms and nap the finished dish with creamy sauce.

Place cutlets between 2 sheets of wax paper. With flat side of a mallet, gently pound until 1/4 inch thick. In a pie pan, mix flour, salt, and pepper. Lightly dust meat with flour mixture.

Heat oil in a wide frying pan over medium-high heat. Add veal and cook until browned on both sides, about 2 minutes on each side. Add wine and cook until alcohol has evaporated. Remove meat from pan and set aside.

Add mushrooms, garlic, and shallot to pan drippings and cook for 2 to 3 minutes. Return meat to pan; add broth. Cover pan and cook for 1 minute. Lift out veal and arrange on a warm serving platter. Spoon mushrooms on top. Add cream to pan drippings. Boil rapidly over high heat until slightly thickened and large shiny bubbles form, 2 to 3 minutes. Pour sauce over veal and mushrooms.

Note: Some oyster mushrooms grow in clusters, other singly, and you need to separate them and trim the bottom of the stems before cutting into thin slices. Tasted raw, oyster mushrooms are disappointing. After a brief saute, their flavor is softened and fully developed.

Grilled Venison Steak

Makes 4 servings

6 tablespoons Thai fish sauce
1/4 cup lemon juice
1 teaspoon crushed dried red chiles
1 teaspoon chopped fresh mint
4 venison steaks, cut 1/2 inch thick

In today's restaurant scene, venison on the menu comes from the ranch, not the range. Farm-raised, the meat is less gamey than its wild counterpart and the flavor is rich and succulent. At California Fats, we "tame" our gourmet game with a quartet of Thai seasonings.

In a wide shallow bowl, combine fish sauce, lemon juice, chiles, and mint. Add steaks and turn to coat both sides. Let meat stand for 15 minutes; turn once or twice during marinating.

Lift meat from marinade and drain briefly. Place the steaks on a greased grill 3 to 4 inches above a solid bed of low-glowing coals. Cook, turning once, for 10 minutes for medium rare or until done to your liking.

Vegetables

Asparagus with Black Bean Sauce

Shiitake Mushrooms with Oyster Sauce

Eggplant in Chile Sauce

Three Mushrooms with Mustard Greens

Baked Stuffed Onions

Herbed Potatoes

Ratatouille

Stuffed Baby Vegetables

Red Beans and Rice

Asparagus with Black Bean Sauce

Makes 4 to 6 servings

2 pounds asparagus
1/4 cup chicken broth
1/4 teaspoon sugar
1 tablespoon sesame oil
2 tablespoons vegetable oil
1/2 medium onion, sliced tip to tip
1 tablespoon minced garlic
*2 tablespoons preserved black beans, rinsed,
    drained, and chopped*
1/2 teaspoon salt
1/8 teaspoon crushed dried red chiles
*1 teaspoon cornstarch dissolved in
    2 teaspoons water*

Asparagus is an important Sacramento Valley crop and we offer it daily during the all-too-short season. Tumbled briefly in a wok, the slender stalks turn a beautiful jade green with a crisp-tender texture. As with any stir-fry, have everything ready before you begin to cook. Slice the asparagus, mix the seasoning sauce, and blend the cornstarch-water thickener. The cooking is so rapid, you need to give it your full attention.

Snap off and discard the tough ends of asparagus; cut spears diagonally into 2-inch pieces. Combine chicken broth, sugar, and sesame oil in a small bowl; set aside.

Heat a wok or wide frying pan over high heat until hot. Add vegetable oil, swirling to coat the sides. Add onion and garlic and stir-fry for 30 seconds. Add asparagus, black beans, salt, and crushed chiles. Stir-fry for 1 minute. Add chicken broth mixture. Cover and cook until asparagus is crisp-tender, about 2 minutes. Add the cornstarch solution and cook, stirring, until sauce boils and thickens slightly.

Note: Small soft preserved black beans are a staple in Cantonese cooking. Rinse the salty coating, then crush the beans to release their pungent flavor before using in a stir-fried dish. After opening, store the beans in an airtight container at room temperature.

Shiitake Mushrooms with Oyster Sauce

Makes 4 to 6 servings

1/2 cup thinly sliced carrot for garnish
  (optional)
1 pound fresh shiitake mushrooms
1 small head Chinese (napa) cabbage
1/2 cup chicken broth
1/4 cup oyster sauce
2 tablespoons soy sauce
1 tablespoon bourbon
2 teaspoons sugar
2 teaspoons sesame oil
2 tablespoons vegetable oil
1 teaspoon cornstarch dissolved in
  2 teaspoons water

Milder tasting than their dried counterparts, fresh shiitake mushrooms give a rich woodsy flavor to this vegetable stir-fry. It makes a distinctive accompaniment to Immigrant's Beef (page 108), Drunk Steak (page 111), or Grilled Venison Steak (page 126).

If using carrot garnish, cook in boiling salted water 2 minutes or until crisp-tender. Drain, rinse with cold water, and set aside. Cut off tough stems from mushrooms (save stems for chicken broth, page 40). Rinse and drain caps; leave caps whole. Trim cabbage; remove outer leaves and save for another use. Cut heart of cabbage lengthwise into quarters. Cook in boiling salted water until tender, 3 to 4 minutes. Drain, rinse with cold water, and drain again; arrange cabbage on a serving platter.

Combine chicken broth, oyster sauce, soy sauce, bourbon, sugar, and sesame oil in a small bowl; set aside.

Heat a wok or wide frying pan over medium-high heat until hot. Add vegetable oil swirling to coat the sides. Add mushrooms and stir-fry for 1 minute. Add chicken broth mixture and cook 3 to 4 minutes or until mushrooms are tender. Add cornstarch solution and cook, stirring, until sauce boils and thickens slightly. With tongs, lift mushrooms from sauce and arrange attractively around cabbage. Pour sauce over all. Garnish with carrot if desired.

Note: Presentation is very important in Chinese cooking so I add carrot slices for color. When I demonstrated this on television I cut the carrot slices into heart shapes using a metal cutter. Over the years I've collected interesting Hong Kong-made cutters—from dragons to flowing-tailed fish.

Eggplant in Chile Sauce

Makes 4 to 6 servings

Garlic-Chile Paste
2 California or New Mexico dried red chiles
4 cloves garlic
3 tablespoons vegetable oil

1/4 cup vegetable oil
1 large eggplant, unpeeled and cut in
  1-inch cubes
2 teaspoons minced garlic
2 teaspoons minced shallot
1 cup chicken broth
1/4 cup soy sauce
1/4 cup rice wine vinegar

*S*ome like it hot, and I like it even hotter in this version of eggplant. To balance the heat, we serve this with steamed rice. If you prefer a milder flavor, don't add the garlic-chile paste all at once, but to taste.

Prepare the paste: Remove stems and seeds from chiles. Place chiles in a pan and cover with water. Cover and simmer 20 minutes or until chiles are very soft; drain. In a blender, puree chiles, garlic, and oil to make a rough paste.

Heat oil in a wide frying pan over medium heat. Add eggplant, garlic, and shallot. Cook, stirring frequently, until eggplant is lightly browned, 4 to 5 minutes. Add garlic-chile paste, chicken broth, soy sauce, and wine vinegar. Cook, uncovered until eggplant is tender and sauce has reduced and thickened, 4 to 5 minutes.

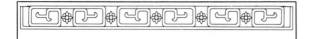

Three Mushrooms with Mustard Greens

Makes 6 to 8 servings

Sauce
1/2 cup chicken broth
3 tablespoons oyster sauce
1 1/2 teaspoons soy sauce
1/2 teaspoon sugar
1/2 teaspoon salt
Pinch of white pepper
1/4 teaspoon sesame oil

12 dried Chinese black mushrooms
1/4 cup sliced carrot, cut in thin diagonal slices
1 can (15 ounces) whole baby corn, drained
1 pound Chinese mustard greens, tough outer
    leaves trimmed, tender leaves sliced
3 tablespoons vegetable oil
1 pound small whole fresh mushrooms,
    stems trimmed
1 can (15 ounces) straw mushrooms, drained
1 teaspoon cornstarch dissolved in
    2 teaspoons water

In this celebrative dish, the three kinds of mushrooms, tiny baby corn, and tender mustard greens taste pure and natural, sweetened with just a hint of oyster sauce. This would good served with Barbecued Pork Loin (page 123) and, because the vegetables are bathed in a clear sauce, steamed rice to soak up the sauce.

Combine sauce ingredients in a small bowl; set aside. Soak dried mushrooms in warm water to cover for 30 minutes; drain. Cut off stems; leave caps whole.

Cook carrot and baby corn in a pan of simmering water for 1 minute; drain. Cook mustard greens in simmering water for 1 minute or just until tender; drain. Arrange mustard greens and corn alternately, spoke-wheel fashion, around the edges of a platter.

Place a wok or wide frying pan over high heat until hot. Add oil, swirling to coat the sides. Add dried mushroom caps and whole fresh mushrooms. Stir-fry for 1 minute. Add straw mushrooms and sauce. Cover and cook until mushrooms are tender, 1 to 2 minutes. Add cornstarch solution and cook, stirring, until sauce boils and thickens slightly. Place mushrooms in center of the platter ringed with mustard greens and corn. Garnish with carrot.

Note: Canned baby corn may be used directly from the can, but we blanch it briefly in water to eliminate any "tinned" taste. We also use this same technique with canned bamboo shoots.

Baked Stuffed Onions

Makes 8 servings

8 medium onions
2 tablespoons olive oil
1 cup chopped raw broccoli
2 cups chopped raw spinach
1/4 teaspoon salt
1/8 teaspoon white pepper
1/8 teaspoon each ground cinnamon, nutmeg,
  and cloves
1/4 cup heavy cream
2 tablespoons chicken broth
1/2 cup crumbled cooked bacon (5 or 6 slices)
1/4 cup dry bread crumbs

On their own, stuffed onions make a handsome vegetable dish to serve on a buffet. Or serve them on either end of a platter to accompany Herbed Standing Rib Roast (page 115) or Garlic Game Hens (page 92).

Peel onions. Using a curved grapefruit knife, cut out a core from the center of each onion leaving a 1/2-inch thick shell. Chop onion centers.

Heat 1 tablespoon of the oil in a wide frying pan over medium heat. Add chopped onion and cook until soft, 4 or 5 minutes. Add broccoli and cook, covered, 2 to 3 minutes or until tender. Stir in spinach and cook, uncovered, 1 to 2 minutes or until spinach is wilted and pan juices have evaporated. Add salt, pepper, cinnamon, nutmeg, and cloves. Stir in cream and chicken broth. Cook until sauce thickens and vegetables are creamy. Stir in bacon.

Stuff onion shells with vegetable mixture. Sprinkle bread crumbs on top. Drizzle the remaining 1 tablespoon oil over crumbs. Place onions in a greased baking pan. Bake, uncovered, in a 375° F oven until onion shells are tender and filling is hot, 20 to 25 minutes.

Herbed Potatoes

Makes 6 servings

*2 pounds red thin-skinned potatoes, peeled and
    cut into quarters*
1/3 cup olive oil
*1/4 cup mixed chopped fresh herbs: basil,
    oregano, and thyme*
1 teaspoon salt
1/2 teaspoon pepper

At California Fats we serve these with our champagne brunch. They make a terrific partner to eggs, but would be just as welcomed for dinner, alongside grilled steak or chicken. If you wish, boil potatoes a day ahead, but give them their crusty finish only minutes before serving.

In a 2 to 3-quart pan, bring 2 inches of water to a boil; add potatoes, cover, and cook until potatoes are tender when pierced, 15 to 20 minutes. Drain. Return pan to low heat and shake 2 or 3 minutes, or until all moisture is evaporated. Let potatoes stand until cool.

Heat oil in a wide frying pan over medium-high heat. Add potatoes to pan. Cook, turning occasionally, until potatoes are lightly browned and crusty, 12 to 15 minutes. Stir in herbs. Season with salt and pepper.

Ratatouille

Makes 6 servings

1 large eggplant, peeled and cut in 1-inch cubes
4 medium zucchini, cut in 1-inch cubes
1 teaspoon salt
1/4 cup olive oil
1 large onion, cut in 1-inch chunks
3 green bell peppers, seeded and cut in
  1-inch squares
3 large tomatoes, peeled and diced
1 teaspoon minced garlic
1/4 cup tomato juice
1 tablespoon dry red wine
1 bay leaf
1 tablespoon chopped parsley
1/2 teaspoon each dried thyme and basil
1/2 teaspoon pepper
Salt
1/2 pound Swiss cheese, sliced (optional)

One of the early recipes at Fat City, this satisfying French vegetable casserole is served as a special during summer and fall when tomatoes are sun-ripened and sweet. You could omit the cheese topping if you wished to serve this as a side dish. For a meal-in-a-bowl, top with bubbly Swiss cheese and pair it with crusty French bread spread with garlic butter (page 61).

Spread eggplant and zucchini on separate paper towels; sprinkle each with half of the 1 teaspoon salt. Let stand 30 minutes. Blot vegetables dry with two more paper towels.

Heat 2 tablespoons of the oil in a 5-quart pan over high heat. Add eggplant and cook until eggplant is lightly browned, 4 to 5 minutes. Remove eggplant from pan. Add the remaining 2 tablespoons oil, zucchini, onion, and bell peppers. Cook over medium heat until onion is soft, 6 to 8 minutes. Return eggplant to pan. Add tomatoes, garlic, tomato juice, wine, bay leaf, parsley, thyme, basil, and pepper. Bring to a boil; reduce heat, cover, and simmer for 30 minutes or until eggplant is very soft. Remove bay leaf; add salt to taste.

If serving with cheese topping, transfer ratatouille to a shallow 2-quart baking dish or six 1 1/2-cup ramekins. Lay cheese slices on top. Broil 4 inches from heat until cheese is bubbly.

Stuffed Baby Vegetables

Makes 4 to 6 servings

1 cup ricotta cheese
3/4 cup grated Parmesan cheese
2 eggs
1/8 teaspooon nutmeg
1/8 teaspoon white pepper
1 cup finely chopped raw spinach leaves
18 baby green zucchini with blossoms
18 baby golden zucchini or baby yellow
    crookneck squash with blossoms
18 cherry tomatoes

*B*ins of tiny blossomed summer squash at our local farmers' market inspired this dish—originally served as part of a tailgate picnic box lunch menu. You can cook the vegetables up to 2 hours ahead: they taste sweetest when served at room temperature.

Combine cheeses, eggs, nutmeg, and white pepper in a bowl; mix well. Stir in spinach; set aside.

Carefully clean squash blossoms; remove the pistil and stamen from each blossom, being careful not to break the blossom from the squash. Wash and stem tomatoes. Cut off a small piece of the tops and remove seeds. Using a pastry bag fitted with a plain tip or a small spoon, stuff cheese mixture into squash blossoms and hollowed tomatoes. Place vegetables in a greased baking pan.

Preheat oven to 350° F. Bake vegetables, uncovered, just until heated through and egg filling is set, 10 to 15 minutes.

Red Beans and Rice

Makes 6 to 8 servings

1 pound dried kidney beans
Cold water
8 cups water
1 ham bone or 1 pound ham shanks
1/2 pound diced cooked ham
1/2 pound Louisiana-style spicy link sausage
1 cup chopped onion
1/4 cup chopped shallots
1/4 cup chopped green bell pepper
1 tablespoon chopped parsley
2 teaspoons minced garlic
1 bay leaf, crumbled
1/4 teaspoon dried thyme
1/4 teaspoon black pepper
Pinch each of dried basil, cayenne, and crushed
*   dried red chiles*
1 1/2 teaspoons salt

steamed rice

Years ago I developed a special menu for Fat City restaurant to celebrate Fat Tuesday, the day before Lent, and we continue to offer it each year. In keeping with the spirit of Mardi Gras, and like dishes served in the Fat City district in New Orleans, the food is redolent with herbs and spices. The smoky flavors of this Cajun classic are well matched by a soft red wine.

Place beans in a large kettle; add enough cold water to cover beans by 2 inches. Cover; bring to a boil over high heat. Boil 2 minutes. Remove from heat; let soak, covered, 1 hour. Drain. Add the 8 cups water and all remaining ingredients except salt. Simmer, partially covered, 2 1/2 to 3 hours or until beans are very tender. At end of cooking, beans should have a little liquid. If beans become too dry, add more water. If beans have more liquid than you like, uncover and boil over medium heat, stirring more frequently as mixture thickens. Remove ham bone; cut meat into bite-size pieces, discarding bone. Return meat to beans. Season beans with salt, and serve over steamed rice.

Desserts

Banana Cream Pie

Rich Pie Pastry

Pecan Pie

Deep-Dish Apple Pies

Persimmon Custard Ginger Tarts

Brandy Apple Tart

Pumpkin Hazelnut Cake

Irish Cream and Pistachio Cheesecake

Bourbon Chocolate Mousse

Chilled Pumpkin Pecan Souffle

Hazelnut Chocolate Zabaglione

Yin Yang Peaches

Spiced Apple Sundaes

Minted Melon Punch

Kiwifruit-Cranberry Punch

Banana Cream Pie

Makes 6 to 8 servings

Rich Pie Pastry for a single-crust 10-inch pie
    (facing page)
3 large eggs
3/4 cup sugar
2 tablespoons cornstarch
1 1/2 tablespoons butter, softened
1 teaspoon vanilla extract
3 1/2 cups milk
4 bananas
1/2 cup heavy cream
1 teaspoon sugar
1/4 teaspoon vanilla extract

*T*his is the legendary Banana Cream Pie served at Frank Fats and California Fats. When I updated our recipes, I kept the filling intact—it had withstood the test of time—but I encased the banana-studded custard in an even flakier, more tender crust.

Preheat oven to 400° F. On a lightly floured board, roll out chilled dough until it is 1/8 inch thick and 2 inches larger in diameter than a 10-inch pie pan. Fit pastry into pan; make a high fluted edge. Prick bottom of pastry in several place with a fork. Place pastry-lined pan in freezer for 30 minutes. Bake in preheated oven 12 to 14 minutes or until lightly browned. Place on a rack and let cool completely before filling.

Prepare the custard: In a medium bowl, beat eggs lightly with an electric mixer. Add sugar, cornstarch, butter, and the 1 teaspoon vanilla; beat until well mixed. In a heavy 3-quart pan, heat milk just to scalding. Pour half of the hot milk into the egg mixture, stirring to blend well. Return egg-milk mixture to remaining milk in pan. Cook, stirring constantly, over low heat until custard has thickened enough to lightly coat a metal spoon. Remove from heat and let custard cool to room temperature.

Peel bananas and cut into 1/4-inch slices, dropping the slices into an even layer over the bottom of the pastry shell. Pour custard over the bananas. Refrigerate for at least 2 hours.

Just before serving, whip cream, sugar, and the 1/4 teaspoon vanilla until stiff. Spread in an even layer over the pie.

Note: If you are using a shallow pie plate, you may have custard and bananas left over. These can be layered in dessert cups and refrigerated.

Rich Pie Pastry

Makes pastry for a single-crust 9 or 10-inch pie
Double recipe for a 2-crust pie

1 cup all purpose flour
1/2 teaspoon sugar
1/2 teaspoon salt
4 tablespoons firm cold butter
4 tablespoons firm cold margarine
3 tablespoons ice water

*T*his pastry has all the right qualities. It is both tender and flaky, it is easy to roll out, and the flavor is delicious. I use it for all sweet pies.

Place flour, sugar, and salt in a food processor fitted with a metal blade. Process 2 seconds. Cut butter and margarine into 1/2-inch chunks and distribute over the flour. Process until fat particles look like small peas, 6 to 8 seconds. With motor running, add ice water through the feed tube. Process just until dough forms a ball.

To make dough without a food processor, combine flour, sugar, and salt in a large bowl. With a pastry blender or two table knives, cut butter and margarine into flour until fat particles look like small peas. While stirring with a fork, sprinkle water over mixture, 1 tablespoon at a time, until all flour is moistened and dough forms a ball.

Shape dough into a 4-inch round; dust with flour. Wrap dough tightly in plastic wrap. Refrigerate for at least 1 hour before using. See specific recipes for baking directions.

Note: You will have to roll the pastry out quite thin in order to make this fit in a 10" deep Pyrex pie plate. If you are in doubt the first time you make this recipe, double it and use the remaining dough for tarts.

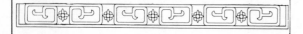

Pecan Pie

Makes 6 to 8 servings

*Rich Pie Pastry for a single-crust
   10-inch pie (page 139)*
4 tablespoons butter, melted and cooled
1/2 cup sugar
1 1/2 tablespoons all-purpose flour
1/4 teaspoon vanilla extract
1/8 teaspoon salt
4 large eggs
1 1/2 cups dark corn syrup
2 1/2 tablespoons dark rum
1 1/2 cups coarsely chopped pecans
10 pecan halves

Sacramento runs a close second to New Orleans as the capitol of jazz, and like the city in the deep south, she celebrates Mardi Gras with gusto. There is a parade, queen, music, and of course good food. During the merriment, Fat City offers southern delights—in keeping with our long tradition of celebrating Fat Tuesday—and you'll find several of these recipes in this book. For dessert, what tastier choice than a rum-spiked pecan-studded pie.

Preheat oven to 350° F. Roll out pastry and line a 10-inch pie pan; flute edges.

In a large bowl, beat together butter, sugar, flour, vanilla, and salt until smooth. Beat in eggs, one at a time. Add corn syrup and rum and mix well. Stir in chopped pecans. Pour filling into pastry shell and arrange pecan halves on top.

Bake on lowest rack of oven until a knife inserted slightly off center comes out clean, 45 to 55 minutes. If pecans on top begin to turn too brown, cover pie loosely with foil. Place on a rack and let cool to room temperature; serve, or refrigerate for up to 24 hours.

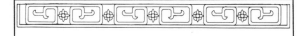

Deep-Dish Apple Pies

Makes 8 individual pies

12 medium sweet-tart apples such as Granny
    Smith or Newtown Pippin
1 3/4 cups sugar
1 tablespoon all-purpose flour
1 tablespoon ground cinnamon
2 teaspoons ground allspice
2 teaspoons ground nutmeg
2 tablespoons lemon juice
1 tablespoon apple schnapps
1 large egg, lightly beaten
3 tablespoons butter, cut into 8 pieces
Rich Pie Pastry for 2 single-crust
    9-inch pies (page 139)
1 large egg lightly beaten with 1 tablespoon milk

*T*here are many options for light fare and snacks on our Fat City menu for diners who prefer to graze with appetizers rather than order an entree. They've told us "all the intriguing choices make it hard to settle on one dish," then added, "plus we want to save room for your great apple pie."

Preheat oven to 450° F. Peel, core, and thinly slice apples to make 12 cups. In a large bowl, combine sugar, flour, cinnamon, allspice, and nutmeg. Add apples, lemon juice, and schnapps; mix well. Stir in lightly beaten egg. Divide the mixture among 8 ramekins, about 1 1/2-cup size. Dot each with a piece of butter.

On a lightly floured board, roll out pastry, half at a time, to about 1/8 inch thick. Cut out 8 circles 1/2 inch larger than the diameter of the ramekins (reroll scraps and cut again if necessary). Drape one pastry circle over each ramekin and fold overhang under. Press edge of pastry with fork tines to make a decorative finish. Cut two gashes in each top; brush with egg-milk mixture.

Bake pies for 10 minutes; reduce oven heat to 350° and bake until apples are tender and pastry is browned, 30 to 40 minutes. Let the pies stand for at least 30 minutes before serving.

Persimmon Custard Ginger Tarts

Makes 12 tarts

Ginger Pastry
2 cups all-purpose flour
1 teaspoon ground ginger
1 teaspoon ground cumin
1/4 teaspoon ground nutmeg
1/4 teaspoon ground cloves
1/4 teaspoon salt
1/2 cup light molasses
1/2 cup unsalted butter, cut in chunks
1/4 cup firmly packed brown sugar
1 large egg, lightly beaten

Persimmon Custard
4 very ripe persimmons
1/4 cup sugar
1/3 cup pear liqueur
2 envelopes unflavored gelatin
1/2 cup cold milk
2 large eggs
1 large egg yolk
1/2 cup sugar
6 tablespoons all-purpose flour
Pinch of salt
1 1/2 cups hot milk
2 teaspoons vanilla extract

2 cups heavy cream
Slivers of peeled persimmon for garnish

*F*or entertaining, you can make these beautiful tarts in stages. First bake the ginger-spiced pastry shells. The morning of the party—or the evening before—make the persimmon filling. Like all gelatin-based mixtures, it needs chilling time to set up.

Prepare the pastry: In a bowl combine flour, ginger, cumin, nutmeg, cloves, and salt; set aside. In a 2-quart pan over low heat, heat molasses until foamy. Remove pan from heat. Add butter, one piece at a time, stirring well after each addition. Add brown sugar and egg; mix well. Add flour mixture, a spoonful at a time, and mix until dough is smooth and shiny. Shape dough into a disk, wrap with plastic wrap, and refrigerate for at least 2 hours.

Preheat oven to 350° F. On a lightly floured board, roll out pastry, half at a time, to about 1/8 inch thick. Cut out 12 six-inch circles (reroll scraps and cut again if necessary). Fit circles into buttered, deep 4-inch tart pans. Prick bottom of each pastry several times with a fork. Bake 10 to 12 minutes or until pastry is lightly browned. Let cool completely before removing shells from pans.

Prepare the custard: Scoop out persimmon flesh; discard skin, seeds, and stems. Whirl flesh in a food processor until smooth. You should have 1 1/2 cups. Place puree in a 2-quart pan with the 1/4 cup sugar and liqueur. Cook, stirring frequently, over medium-low heat until mixture becomes very thick, 5 to 10 minutes. Remove from heat and set aside.

In a small bowl, sprinkle gelatin over cold milk; let soften for several minutes. In a heavy 2-quart pan, whisk whole eggs, egg yolk, and the 1/2 cup sugar until mixture thickens and turns pale yellow. Whisk in flour and salt. Gradually whisk in hot milk. Cook over medium-low heat, stirring constantly, until custard has thickened enough to lightly coat a metal spoon. Remove from heat; add softened gelatin and stir until dissolved. Stir in vanilla. Refrigerate until custard mounds slightly when dropped from a spoon.

Fold persimmon puree into chilled custard. Whip cream until it holds soft peaks, then fold into custard. Spoon filling into tart shells. Refrigerate until firm, 3 to 4 hours. Before serving, garnish each tart with slivers of persimmon.

Note: This filling should be made with Hachiya-type persimmons—the pointy-shaped ones most commonly sold commercially and grown in home gardens. Use fully ripened persimmons; unripe ones have an astringent flavor. If the fruit feels hard, let it stand at room temperature for a few days until it becomes very soft and sweet.

Brandy Apple Tart

Makes 8 servings

Shortbread Pastry
3 1/2 tablespoons butter
2 tablespoons shortening
1/2 cup sugar
1 large egg
1/4 teaspoon vanilla extract
1 3/4 cups all-purpose flour
1 tablespoon unsweetened cocoa
1/4 teaspoon baking powder
1/4 teaspoon baking soda

Custard
3 large eggs
1 cup milk
1/4 cup sugar
2 tablespoons apple schnapps
Pinch of ground allspice

Apple Glaze
3/4 cup sugar
3/4 cup apple schnapps
1/2 cup water
Pinch of ground allspice
2 medium Granny Smith or Newton Pippin
    apples peeled, cored, and thinly sliced
2 teaspoons arrowroot mixed with 2 table-
    spoons apple schnapps

Sweetened whipped cream spiced with a pinch of
    ground cinnamon (optional)

*P*art of the pleasure in baking is making a beautiful, and sometimes unexpected, presentation. To celebrate Saint Valentine's Day, I bake this luscious tart in a heart-shaped pan. No matter what shape you use, for a professional finish, take time to arrange the apple slices in neat overlapping layers on top of the custard.

Preheat oven to 350° F. In large bowl of an electric mixer, beat butter, shortening, and sugar until creamy. Beat in egg and vanilla. Add flour, cocoa, baking powder, and baking soda. Mix until dough forms a ball. On a lightly floured board, roll out pastry to 1/8 inch thick and line an 11-inch tart pan with a removable bottom or a 10-inch quiche dish; trim pastry even with pan rim.

Prepare the custard: In a medium bowl, slightly beat eggs with a wire whisk. Whisk in milk, sugar, schnapps, and allspice, blending until smooth. Pour into pastry shell. Bake until a knife inserted in center comes out clean, 30 to 40 minutes. Place on a rack and let cool. When cold, remove pan sides if using tart pan with a removable bottom.

Prepare the glaze: In a 2-quart pan, combine sugar, schnapps, water, and allspice. Cook over medium heat, stirring occasionally, until sugar is disssolved. Add apples to pan and simmer 2 to 3 minutes or until apples are barely soft but still retain their shape. With a slotted spoon, lift apples from syrup and drain in a colander. Add arrowroot mixture to syrup and cook, stirring, until glaze thickens slightly.

To assemble tart, arrange apples attractively on the custard filling; brush generously with glaze. Offer the remaining glaze and cinnamon whipped cream at the table to spoon over each serving.

Pumpkin Hazelnut Cake

Makes 8 to 10 servings

1 3/4 cups unsifted cake flour
2 teaspoons ground cinnamon
1 teaspoon ground nutmeg
1 teaspoon ground cloves
1 teaspoon baking powder
1/2 teaspoon salt
3 large eggs
1 1/4 cups firmly packed brown sugar
9 tablespoons olive oil
3 tablespoons walnut oil
1 1/2 cups canned pumpkin
1 cup coarsely chopped hazelnuts

Chocolate Hazelnut Glaze
3 ounces semi-sweet chocolate, chopped
1 tablespoon heavy cream
1 tablespoon hazelnut-flavor liqueur

*T*his cake is not overly rich, but the pureed pumpkin helps it retain moisture and a fresh-baked taste for several days. For the oil, I use California-produced walnut oil for its nutty flavor and virgin olive oil for its neutral quality. Splendid in other cooking, extra virgin olive oil has a too-intense flavor for this recipe.

Preheat oven to 300° F. Spray a 10-inch bundt pan or a 6-cup mold with cooking spray, dust with flour, and set aside. Sift together flour, cinnamon, nutmeg, cloves, baking powder, and salt; set aside.

In large bowl of an electric mixer, beat eggs and brown sugar until well blended. Add olive oil and walnut oil and beat slowly until very smooth. Beat in pumpkin; gradually beat in dry ingredients until all flour has been incorporated. Stir in nuts. Spoon batter into prepared pan. Bake for 40 minutes or until a wooden pick inserted in center comes out clean. Let cake cool in pan on wire rack for 10 minutes, then turn out onto rack to cool completely.

Place chocolate, cream, and liqueur in a small pan. Cook over low heat until chocolate melts and glaze has reduced to a syrup consistency, 3 to 4 minutes. Drizzle glaze over cake. Let glaze stand a few minutes to set up.

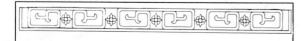

Irish Cream and Pistachio Cheesecake

Makes 10 servings

Pistachio Crust

*1 cup chocolate wafer crumbs (about
    20 wafers)*
3 tablespoons finely chopped pistachio nuts
2 tablespoons powdered sugar
1 1/2 teaspoons ground cinnamon
4 tablespoons clarified butter (page 109)

Filling

*1 1/2 pounds fresh cream cheese or 3 packages
    (8 ounces each) cream cheese, softened*
*1 cup plus 2 tablespoons firmly packed
    dark brown sugar*
3 large eggs
1/3 cup Irish coffee liqueur
1 1/2 tablespoons espresso liqueur
1 tablespoon cold strong espresso coffee
1/2 teaspoon vanilla extract

Topping

1 cup heavy cream
1 1/2 teaspoons sugar
1 teaspoon cold strong espresso coffee
Whole peeled pistachio nuts

*H*ere is an updated version of a grand old-fashioned cheesecake for a grand celebration—Saint Patrick's Day—or any time you want to celebrate with friends. One of our dessert suppliers liked the cheesecake so well he asked for permission to use the recipe to retail the cake in his bakery.

Preheat oven to 325° F. In a bowl, combine crumbs, nuts, powdered sugar, and cinnamon; stir in butter. Press mixture firmly over the sides and bottom of a greased 9-inch spring form pan. Bake for 8 minutes. Place on a rack and let cool.

In large bowl of an electric mixer, beat cream cheese and brown sugar until soft and smooth. With mixer on lowest speed, beat in eggs, one at a time. Add liqueurs, coffee, and vanilla; beat just until smooth (do not overbeat). Pour filling into prepared crust and bake in a 325° F oven until center is slightly puffed and a knife inserted in center comes out clean, 1 1/4 to 1 1/2 hours. Place on a rack and let cool to room temperature, then cover and refrigerate until well chilled.

To serve, remove pan sides and place cake on a platter. Whip cream, sugar, and coffee until stiff. Spread a thin layer of cream on top of cheesecake. Pipe cream rosettes around edge of cake and place nuts attrractively in the center.

Note. For a perfectly smooth cheesecake, you must mix slowly. If too much air is whipped into the batter, the cheesecake may crack. It will still taste delicious, and any possible cracks won't show after you complete the decorative finish.

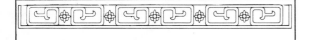

Bourbon Chocolate Mousse

Makes 8 servings

1 pound semi-sweet chocolate, chopped
4 tablespoon unsalted butter, cut in chunks
1 cup heavy cream
4 large egg yolks
1 cup powdered sugar
1 cup bourbon

Raspberry Sauce
1 cup raspberries
1/2 cup water
1/4 cup sugar
1 tablespoon raspberry liqueur

Raspberry Cream
1 cup heavy cream
1/4 cup raspberry sauce (above)

Mousse is not an everyday dessert so I think it's worthwhile to give it a splashy presentation. Pour the chocolate mixture in a mold and chill it overnight. After unmolding the mousse, pipe pink raspberry-cream rosettes around the base, and serve with raspberry sauce. A chocoholics dream come true!

In the top of a double boiler, melt chocolate and butter with cream over simmering water. Remove the top pan. One at a time, beat egg yolks into chocolate mixture. Sift powdered sugar; add to chocolate mixture and stir until smooth. Stir in bourbon. Smoothly line a 6-cup mold with plastic wrap. Pour mousse into the mold. Cool to room temperature, then refrigerate, covered, overnight.

Prepare the sauce: In a 2-quart pan, combine raspberries, water, and sugar. Cook over medium heat, stirring occasionally, until sugar is dissolved. Simmer, uncovered, 10 to 15 minutes or until sauce thickens slightly. Strain sauce through a fine sieve; stir in liqueur. Refrigerate until needed.

To serve, unmold mousse onto a cake plate; slowly peel off plastic wrap. Whip cream until stiff; fold in 1/4 cup of the raspberry sauce. Pipe raspberry cream rosettes around base of the mousse. Serve remaining raspberry sauce on the side.

Chilled Pumpkin Pecan Souffle

Makes 6 to 8 servings

1 1/2 tablespoons unflavored gelatin
1/4 cup cold water
1 cup sugar
1/2 cup water
1 teaspoon grated orange peel
1 can (16 ounces) pumpkin
3 tablespoon orange juice
1/2 cup finely chopped pecans
6 large egg whites
1/4 teaspoon cream of tartar
1 cup heavy cream
Whipped cream rosettes and pecan halves

Not only will this souffle not fall, you should make it a day ahead—a boon when entertaining. I developed the recipe originally for television and now it's part of our catering menu.

Cut a piece of wax paper long enough to wrap around a 1 1/2-quart souffle dish. Fold paper in half lengthwise. Wrap around dish to make a 3-inch collar. Tie paper around dish with string, brush the inside of the paper with vegetable oil, and set aside.

In a small bowl, sprinkle gelatin over the 1/4 cup cold water; let soften for several minutes. In a 2-quart pan, combine 1/2 cup of the sugar, the 1/2 cup water, and orange peel. Cook over medium heat, stirring occasionally, until sugar is dissolved. Add softened gelatin and stir until dissolved. Let cool slightly, then stir in pumpkin and orange juice until evenly blended. Stir in pecans.

In large bowl of an electric mixture, beat egg whites and cream of tartar until frothy. Add the remaining 1/2 cup sugar, 1 tablespoon at a time, beating well after each addition. Continue to beat until sugar is dissolved and meringue holds glossy stiff peaks. In another bowl, whip cream until it holds soft peaks. Fold pumpkin mixture into meringue, then fold in whipped cream. Spoon into prepared dish. Refrigerate until firm, about 4 hours, or for up to 24 hours.

Just before serving, remove paper collar from dish. Garnish top of souffle with whipped cream rosettes and pecan halves.

Note: Egg whites whip to greater volume when they are at room temperature. Place unshelled eggs in a bowl, cover with lukewarm water, and let stand 15 minutes. Dry eggs before separating the whites from the yolks.

Hazelnut Chocolate Zabaglione

Makes 4 servings

1 cup strawberries, hulled and halved
4 kiwifruit, peeled and quartered
2 tablespoons hazelnut-flavor liqueur
1 tablespoon sugar
1/2 cup hazelnuts

Zabaglione
4 large egg yolks
1 tablespoon sugar
1/4 cup hazelnut-flavor liqueur
1 tablespoon heavy cream
1 tablespoon brandy
1 teaspoon lemon juice
2 tablespoons (1 ounce) white chocolate, melted
1 tablespoon (1/2 ounce) semi-sweet
*   chocolate, melted*

Oregon hazelnuts and California-grown straw-berries and kiwifruit give a fresh new look to Italian zabaglione. You must make this frothy dessert just before serving, but you can make it in minutes. It will be ready before guests have finished their first cup of coffee.

In a bowl, toss strawberries and kiwifruit with liqueur and sugar. Divide the mixture among four dessert goblets, cover, and refrigerate for 2 hours for flavors to blend. Place hazelnuts in a pie pan. Bake in a 350° F oven until golden brown, about 15 minutes. Let nuts cool, then chop and set aside.

Prepare the zabaglione: In the top of a double boiler, beat together egg yolks, sugar, liqueur, cream, brandy, lemon juice, and melted chocolates. Set double boiler top over simmering water. Whip mixture constantly with a wire whip or electric mixer until foam is just thick enough to briefly hold a peak when whip is withdrawn, 5 to 7 minutes. The volume will triple or quadruple. Immediately pour zabaglione over fruit in dessert goblets, sprinkle with nuts, and serve.

Note: When I studied at the Culinary Institute of America we made zabaglione the classical way, beating the egg yolk-wine mixture with a balloon whisk. It takes a strong arm to whisk continuously for five minutes or more! These days I use a portable electric mixer to give zabaglione its fluffy light volume.

Yin Yang Peaches

Makes 4 servings

*1/2 cup unsalted macadamia nuts, cut
    into halves*
4 peaches
1/4 cup sugar
1/4 teaspoon ground allspice

Citrus Sauce
2 cups fresh orange juice
1 cup fresh grapefruit juice
1 cup fresh lemon juice
1/4 cup honey

Raspberry-wildberry Sauce
1 cup raspberries
1/2 cup water
1/4 cup sugar
1 tablespoon wildberry-flavor liqueur

*T*hough taste and eye appeal were foremost when I developed this recipe, the presentation resembled the Chinese concept of yin and yang—the idea of two opposing forces in balance. Here a tangy citrus sauce is contrasted by a sweet raspberry sauce, the two providing a flavorful balance for summer peaches.

Place nuts in a pie pan. Bake in a 350° F oven, shaking pan once, until lightly browned, 12 to 15 minutes. Set nuts aside and increase oven temperature to 400° F.

Blanch peaches in a pan of boiling water 2 minutes. Drain and rinse with cold water to cool. Slip off skins, halve peaches, and remove pits. Place peaches in a lightly greased baking pan. Combine sugar and allspice; sprinkle over peaches. Bake for 12 to 15 minutes or until peaches are tender but still hold their shape. Let stand until cool.

In a 2-quart pan, combine orange juice, grapefruit juice, lemon juice, and honey. Bring to a boil over medium heat. Simmer, uncovered, until sauce is reduced to 2 cups, about 10 minutes. Let cool, then refrigerate until needed.

In another pan, combine raspberries, water, and sugar. Cook over medium heat, stirring occasionally, until sugar is dissolved. Simmer, uncovered, 10 to 15 minutes or until sauce thickens slightly. Strain sauce through a fine sieve; stir in liqueur. Let cool, then refrigerate until needed.

To assemble spoon citrus sauce on 4 rimmed dessert plates. Ladle about 1/4 cup raspberry-wildberry sauce over one side of citrus sauce. Place 2 peach halves on each plate where the two sauces join. Sprinkle nuts on top.

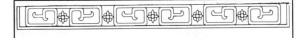

Spiced Apple Sundaes

Makes 4 to 6 servings

4 large Newtown Pippin or Granny
   Smith apples
1/2 cup butter
2/3 cup light corn syrup
2 tablespoons firmly packed brown sugar
1 teaspoon lemon juice
1/2 teaspoon ground mace
1/2 teaspoon ground allspice
1/4 teaspoon ground cardamom
1 quart vanilla ice cream

No matter how tempting our dessert selection, there is always someone whose favorite is ice cream. It becomes a special treat when topped with warm spiced apples.

Peel, core, and thinly slice apples. You should have 4 cups. Melt butter in a wide frying pan over medium heat. When butter is bubbly, add apples. Cook, stirring occasionally, until apples are tender but still hold their shape, about 5 minutes. Add corn syrup, brown sugar, lemon juice, mace, allspice, and cardamom. Stir gently to combine all ingredients. Heat until mixture comes to a boil; cook for 1 or 2 minutes, then remove from heat. To serve, place one or two scoops of ice cream in each dessert bowl. Top with warm apple topping.

The Fragrant Spices

William Cowper, in his poem, *The Task* (1783), wrote: "Variety is the very spice of life." And a variety of spices gives new life to cooking.

Mace, the covering between the husk and the seed of the nutmeg, imparts a warm spicy flavor similar to nutmeg, but slightly more pugent. Allspice is the dried berry of a West Indian tree. It combines the flavors of cinnamon and cloves. Cardamom, one of the oldest spices known to man, is the aromatic seed of a plant belonging to the ginger family. It is especially popular in Scandinavian and Indian cookery for its sweet pungency. Ground mace and ground allspice are widely available, while cardamom is usually sold in the pod. To grind cardamom, crack open the soft, ivory colored pods and crush the seeds with a mortar and pestle or grind in an electric spice grinder.

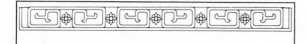

Minted Melon Punch

Makes about 32 1/2-cup servings

Ice Ring
1/2 cup plus 2 tablespoons wildberry schnapps
3 tablespoons blueberry schnapps
2 tablespoons peppermint schnapps
4 cups (about 1 liter) 7-Up
1/2 honeydew melon, scooped into balls
1/2 cantaloupe, scooped into balls
8 strawberries, hulled and thinly sliced
2 lemons, thinly sliced crosswise
2 limes, thinly sliced crosswise
Fresh edible flowers

6 tablespoons melon-flavor liqueur
4 tablespoons wildberry schnapps
2 tablespoons peppermint schnapps
3 quarts plus 3 cups (about 4 liters)
*   7-Up, chilled*

*G*raduations, bridal showers, and weddings keep our catering department busy, especially in spring and summer. One of our most popular punches is laced with fruit-flavored schnapps and liqueur. We use full-sized bottles from our inventory, but you can buy small bottles containing about 1/4 cup each at a well-stocked wine shop.

Prepare the ice ring; in a large pitcher or bowl combine the three kinds of schnapps and 7-Up. Arrange half of the fruits and flowers in the bottom of a 1 1/2-quart ring mold. Cover with one-fourth of the 7-Up mixture. Freeze. Add the rest of the fruits and flowers; cover with the remaining 7-Up mixture. Freeze again. When frozen solid, cover mold with foil.

Just before serving, place the three kinds of schnapps and 7-Up in a punch bowl; stir gently to mix. Place ice ring in a pan of warm water to release from the mold. Float ice ring in the punch.

Kiwifruit–Cranberry Punch

Makes about 30 1/2-cup servings

1/2 cup fresh lemon juice
1/4 cup sugar
1/4 cup brandy
1/4 cup cherry brandy
1/4 cup orange liqueur
2 bottles (750 ml each) champagne, chilled
2 quarts (about 2 liters) carbonated water or
    use equal parts carbonated water and
    7-Up, chilled
Ice cubes
1 cup cranberries
6 kiwifruit, peeled and sliced

*T*oast the holiday season with this colorful not-too-sweet punch.

In a 2-cup glass measure, combine lemon juice, sugar, brandies, and liqueur. Stirring occasionally, let stand until sugar is dissolved. Chill until ready to use.

Just before serving, place brandy mixture in a punch bowl. Add champagne and carbonated water. Stir gently to mix. Float ice cubes on top of punch. Float cranberries and kiwifruit slices on top of ice cubes.

INDEX

T

The Crossing Press

publishes a full line of cookbooks.
For a free catalog, call toll-free
1-800-777-1048.
Please specify a *cookbook* catalog.